BUSH BROTHER

1534

£8

BUSH BROTHER

Written and Illustrated
by

Graham Jeffery

WOLFE PUBLISHING LTD
10 Earlham Street London WC 2

By the same Author:
Barnabas
More Barnabas
Even More Barnabas
Barnabas Comes Fourth

With acknowledgement to the B.B.C. for permission to use the two 'sermonettes', if that is the word, which form the pro. and the epi. logue of this book.

Printed in Great Britain by
Morrison and Gibb Ltd., London and Edinburgh

Contents

7

Dedication

For the brothers of S. Barnabas and my
little parish of S. Peter's, Collinsville,
whom . . . among others . . . I shall
probably never forget.

Preface

This is really what A. A. Milne calls the um-er part of the book: where the speaker clears his throat, and wonders, anxiously, what on earth he is to say.

I am a little in that position. For I have never written a book before (though I have drawn a few) and the only excuse I have for this one is that I've been asked to. Really, I was only going to do the pictures. But that left us with the problem of forming a committee to write the words. And committees, as you know, rarely achieve anything. It was not a committee, for instance, that saved the world. A committee wasn't even formed for the Creation. Can you imagine the chaos if there had been? One member, for example, to another angel, showing a rough draft of the Himalayas: "do you think we could get planning permission for this lot?"

No: it's best to stick to the memories of one man, however unworthy. And so I've just used my own letters home, which my mother happily (or perhaps not?) hung on to. I've expanded them occasionally. But more often I've shortened them: especially when the references are solely personal, about my parents for instance: or about Anthony & Juliet; or our dog Harper (who, you may be sure, barked furiously whenever one of these letters arrived).

So there you are. They are poor things, written shakily at my Rectory desk, with a sweaty hand. The temperature is around 100°. Little geckoes are running about on the ceiling above my head. (They've married and a whole family of them look out for Mosquitoes which they catch, remarkably quickly, with

their tongues.) Even so, I need a Mosquito coil burning by my side, to save me from being eaten alive.

So far as I can tell, there have been various Bush brotherhoods in Australia for about seventy years. That of the 'Good Shepherd', in New South Wales, is probably the best known:

10

along with our own 'S. Barnabas' in N. Queensland. But there are, and have been, smaller brotherhoods whose work is just the same: to look after the church in the Outback. In fact, most of the St. Barnabas Brothers work at two Brotherhood schools: and only 3 or 4 are 'bush parsons' so to speak, travelling vast distances as in the old days (though by car, not horse, this time!). But this is because, like everyone else, they are short of clergy. So that my own (conceited word that!) little parish of Collinsville has a brother no longer.

I joined the brotherhood more or less by mistake. I had finished 3 tiring years in Southampton (parish of 30,000) when I sat next to Ian Shevill, N. Queensland's Bishop, at supper in Bognor Regis where my father is a dentist. He said N. Queensland was short of clergy, so I said I'd go. Which is why I wrote these letters home.

But since I wasn't born with a collar round my neck (very few of us are) I thought I'd begin this little bundle of memories with an incident which didn't happen when I was in the pulpit, or even at the altar step . . . but simply one rather shy member of a (for once) huge congregation. . . .

I was sitting with my friend Bobby, another theological student, up near the front. And we waited for our friend Ken to be ordained. Just before the actual ordination began, a priest walked to the front of the church, knelt down, and announced that he would sing the Litany. (You know, that rather long series of prayers, asking God to bless the sick, women in child-birth, travellers . . . in fact, all God's children.) So the priest knelt down and began to chant the opening prayer "O God the Father of Heaven, have mercy upon us, miserable sinners".

And then there was an awkward silence, because I didn't sing, and Bobby didn't sing, and no one else had the courage to either. So the priest carried on with the next petition all on his own, "O God the Son, Redeemer of the world, have mercy upon us . . ."

Well, I've said no one joined in. And that was certainly what I thought at the time. But as the Litany continued, I realised I was wrong. For I could just hear a frail sound coming from the old lady beside me. She was—though no one else could possibly have heard it—singing. A very frail squeaky voice it was, and I must say at once that the old lady had a deaf aid. And probably was only singing because she assumed everyone else was too.

Well, it was a duet then, and for some verses the rather strange duet went on. "That it may please Thee to bless and keep all thy people", the little old lady beside me replying, "We beseech Thee to hear us, Good Lord". And then I heard another sound from my other side. A little sort of humming sound it was, not very tuneful. And I realised to my shame that Bobby was beginning to join the chorus. I tried to then, only very half-heartedly I must confess, in case I should be heard. So it was that by ones and twos people began to pluck up courage and join in. And when at last the time came for the priest to sing, "O Lamb of God that takest away the sins of the World", the whole congregation, hundreds strong, replied as one man, "Grant us Thy peace".

Now the Song that you and I sing, if ever we go to church, is one of praise to God. And this is a Song in which millions join. But it wasn't always like that. It started with one man, and his name was Jesus of Nazareth, whose whole life was an act of praise to God. And then there were the others who joined him and took up the Song: Peter and Andrew and James and Mary Magdalene. And then others joined *them*—Paul of Tarsus and Timothy, for instance. And then *you* joined them, and it may be—me. Where one man alone had offered up his life to God, millions and millions have now joined in: trying to sing the same song. And Christians look forward to the time when not just millions, not just all mankind, but all creation will join in Christ's song to God. And the earth will be filled with the knowledge of the Lord—as the waters cover the sea.

My Dear

Well, here I am in Australia! A very friendly reception at the airport. "Hallo there, Father," said a Customs Official. "So you've come to join us, have you?" He then put a white cross with his chalk on my solitary suitcase (symbolic this?) and led me

through the barrier. So I'm in. Though I must say I find it rather hot: a change from saying goodbye to you two days ago in London Airport. I was glad, and grateful, for the good facilities here. Soap, towel, and key to the shower room, all free on request. So I got straight into a cold shower!

Yungabar, by contrast, is not so nice. Bit of a shock really. Lying on my bed in a dormitory, divided bed from bed by wooden partitions (with the folk next door swearing twenty to the dozen). I thought I was back in my National service barrack room. But today I'm a bit more cheerful. Another Bush brother (Derek) has arrived, and we set off for Ravenshoe in a couple of days. The food here is tolerable, and there's a large community wash-room. Also the inevitable "old boy", who's been in Australia six weeks, and spends his hours telling the rest of us how he's been shooting crocodiles up in the Gulf. I don't know if anyone believes him. . . .

It's one o'clock on Sunday morning, and you are still in bed I hope: while we stretch our legs in Rockhampton Station. (This by the way is the dividing line. From now on we are in the

Tropics.) On the other side of the platform the trains look like this with "Women and Children only" on the carriage doors. The air-conditioned "Sunlander" seems hot at night: but almost blissfully cold by comparison with the outside. So, for two days, we wend our way some 1,000 miles and more up the Queensland coast. To catch a bus tomorrow afternoon which will take us inland from Innisfail to Ravenshoe.

There's a gospel hall further up, along the track. Wooden, up on its stilts, as all the other houses. I still haven't seen a kangaroo. Nor a koala bear, which we are unlikely to see. Nor a crocodile, which do indeed dwell here in numbers, but further up even from Ravenshoe.

Here's another snatch of Australia, glimpsed thru' (as they say) another compartment window. With each house is a tank for water. Which you wouldn't like, because it's tasteless; at least so far.

The train travels very slowly. About 20 mph for much of the time, and I'm always thinking it's due to stop. But it doesn't . . . it just goes on and on.

N.B. I never did see a koala bear: until the time came for me to leave Australia, and my friend Philip took me to a Koala Sanctuary in Sydney. Here, with notices saying 'Koala' everywhere, we wandered for what seemed like ages before at last we caught sight of one, sitting happily on a branch high, high up: and chewing, I imagine, eucalyptus leaves.

As for turtles, I don't think I ever spotted one. Though Basil, in our bathes at Little Milly, was forever seeing them. And partly I believe him. Though it was bubbles coming up and the imagination of gurgles fading below that I think attracted him.

Anyway, wherever I invariably swam up to him, they had invariably gone.

19 Dec Ravenshoe.

It seems a long time since I wrote to you, and I'm not quite sure where I got to. We got to Innisfail all right: sharing a sleeper with a boy from Charters Towers (the other Brotherhood school) and I had the middle bunk.

The only trouble was an Australian who was too friendly, and kept telling us things for what seemed like hours (and as you know, I always speak to my companions in a Railway compartment myself. But not to this extent).

17

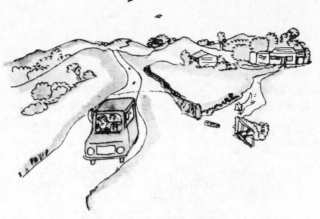

Derek and I travelled by Dormobile from Innisfail to R'hoe. Neville the driver delivers the newspapers to those who live along the way by throwing them out of the window, and over the van. Even so they arrive in the right garden. In one house a dog ran down to greet him, carrying the paper home in its mouth.

The rain here is heavy. It looks as if a storm is brewing now. It will beat down so hard that the drain pipes will pour water not downwards onto the ground, but sideways in a heavy spurt. Like this.

You wouldn't like the roads, Dad. Some are reasonable, but even these do not permit of overtaking without going onto the hard earth at the side of the road. Robert, the headmaster, came out to greet us: covered in mud. He'd been milking the cows.

I'm sorry this will have to serve as my Christmas greeting. While you shiver, I bake "and which is worse I know not: but I know that both are ill".

Tell Anthony I saw some Ibis (birds) today. Also cockroaches, so big, but harmless. The spiders are very artful though. They build their webs (even a thread is relatively strong) around the outside lamps. They know that the moths and flies are attracted by the light, so they come out at night!

Dec 26 Boxing Day Ravenshoe

Have just been to Milla Milla (Aborigine for water water) spent Saturday night there, a few feet from the altar (behind a curtain). I woke to ring the bell at 6.30 a.m. for the 7.00. And after breakfast to ring at 9.30 for the 10 o'clock. About 15 came to the first, 7 to the second. The toilet adjoining the church proved so repulsive, that I sought refuge elsewhere: with Mr. & Mrs. Hall whose house is next door. They also gave me tea and toast, and a nice calendar I've sent to you sea-mail. I'm sorry to be so earthy, but these outback closets are the limit. Already I find myself longing for the "flush-pots" of Europe.

"CERTAINLY YOU CAN
COME ON INSIDE"

Basil, who describes his life as a 'tale of three cities', is the local Brother here. And I'm to look after his 'parish' while he goes on holiday later. We spent Christmas Eve at Milla itself. With 40 at Midnight Mass. Before that we had Evensong and Blessing of the Crib at R'hoe (16 miles away) and afterwards went back the 16 miles for the 7 a.m. service. Then 30 miles to Mt. Garnet for the 10 o'clock service, then back here for a party at 6.30 p.m. Sorry if I've muddled you.

My Christmas lunch was an endurance test. I left the table twice to have a cold shower. Even so, the pace of life is immeasurably slower here. My day at Milla was easiest: with meals arranged at different families, one of whom took me to see Lake Eacham. Here I saw a notice saying 'Turtles', thus adding another mammal to the list of those I have not seen.

Since 1963 totters wearily to its close, I thought I'd write at least one letter on white paper, and blow the expense. Especially as the air-mail paper gets tedious after a while. Also it gives me a chance to draw one or two pictures. First, S. Barnabas Church, Ravenshoe . . .

And here is a rough impression of S. Barnabas School. Wooden, on stilts, with cows munching by day and spiders waiting at night. Always the same ones in the same place. But the flies do not decrease, noticeably. One thread, perhaps two on inspection, will bind a cobweb some 15 ft up to the ground.

Played tennis on Saturday with Eddie W.S., Labour M.P. for Ravenshoe district in the State Parliament. But I'm afraid I won't get a chance to do so again. Little Susan Tilt from our Sunday School wrote me this charming letter. "Dear Brother Graham.

Mrs. Wallis Smith has told Eddie he is not to play with you again. It's not good for him. When he got back, he was completely exhorsted. . . ."

'Completely exhorsted'

The collection on Sunday morning from a congregation of eleven was £63. 17. 1d. Rather excessive I thought. But one person had paid by envelopes, no doubt for a period of time; which partly expiates this excess!

Mrs. Frost, whom I visited out 'bush', has a kangaroo called 'Wally'. At least, he lives wild: but comes up when she calls him to receive a bun or so for 'smoko' (elevenses) over the fence.

R'hoe 18 Jan 1964

Still visiting the children's families. A lady said to me "You're not English, are you? Well you don't sound like one. You must be one of the civilised ones". I'm not quite sure how to take this.

R'hoe 27 Jan 64

Thank you for the Diary, Juliet. My first entry was made during our Chapter Meeting on Friday: when all the brothers were gathered together. I'm to go to Collinsville, a township of around 2,000: which hasn't had a resident Anglican Minister since 1940. It's fairly near Townsville (180 miles is fairly near by Australian standards).

N.B. My 1940 predecessor, 'dear old Mr Mead who had a dog': I never gathered any more information about him than this.

Basil is away, so I am as they say 'in charge'. Partly 'baching' (i.e. doing for myself) down at the Rectory: but far far more often being invited out or eating up at the school. The boys are back: and a look at my diary says I hardly miss a day under the waterfall at Little Milly.

P.S. At last I am able to jump off the top rock, which took me 18 swims or so to achieve: but the children do it easily.

When the wet arrives, the 'fall' at the far end, which you can just get under now, becomes a torrent: and you can get nowhere near it, being swept continually with great force to this end.

I suppose I should draw you a picture, verbally and visually, of my little week-end place here. The vestry is made up into a bedroom: in the sense that it has a bed. But unfortunately Basil's been told that it's healthy to sleep on a hard bed. I should like to get my hands on the propagator of this beastly idea. Alas! Basil has done his job well. A table top is securely fastened to the bed, and the thin mattress doesn't help enough to let me get off to sleep.

The vestry is also a kitchen, in that you can boil a pot of tea. And the cupboard, where the tea and sugar are kept, is full of cockroaches. Harmless creatures really, I spend half the night not sleeping: and half throwing my sandals at them. There's also a shower. But use it before nightfall, in case of snakes. . . .

You need to be careful in the morning, that you dress before entering the church. It's easy to peep in, still in pyjamas, and deflect early arrivals from their prayers!

Two little girls were waiting patiently for me outside the closet: which was slightly less beastly than that at Milla Milla. "Is there Sunday School, Brother Graham?" they asked. I did not expect any but said "Why not?" So they ran and fetched Judith, thus making four of us.

I visit some little Aborigine children here, most unsuccessfully. They just keep on laughing at my beard!

I took Holy Communion recently at a local farmstead, on the way to Milla Milla. "I'm afraid Dora's arrived" said Mrs. M. as she opened the door (or would have done if there'd been one) "so I hope you won't mind celebrating inside, instead of on the verandah." "How nice," I replied, assuming Dora to be her daughter. But though I delayed a bit, she never turned up. I did not like to press the point. Perhaps she was a strict Methodist? So I celebrated for the three of us, in their inside room: but my thoughts kept wandering to Dora, who I could just hear, as she seemed to potter about on the verandah. In front of me, through their window, I could see the rolling hills. It was one

27

of my first outback communions, and I only wished that their daughter could have joined us.

Afterwards, at breakfast, I asked where Dora was: as she still had not appeared. "Ah brother" said Mrs. M. "I thought you didn't understand". . . . Dora was of course a Cyclone!

On the way back I stopped to teach at Minbun: a little outback school for fourteen children, who assemble at the sound of a whistle. And march to gramophone music into their classroom.

Also visit C. who is supposedly on the point of death: but turns out to be a darn sight fitter than I am. Later, after a long winding search, I find a girl whose little daughter Suzanne was killed by a Stinger jellyfish at Cairns recently. She seemed grateful for the visit, which I must try to repeat, whenever I'm this way again. The Stinger, by the way, seems more dangerous than the crocodile or snake or anything else.

I have had, also, my first taste of regular teaching in the State School. Open doors, noisy corridors, forty children at a time, four lessons in one and three-quarter hours, with the voice of neighbouring teachers filtering through. A lady teacher, whose harassed face I glimpsed from the corridor, gave me my first glimpse of a person in front of a firing squad. Tense, harassed, screaming short commands to keep back that advancing tide of inattention, fidgeting and mumbling, which creepeth ever forward.

Then came my own baptism of fire!

Ravenshoe March 64.

We were four at Communion this morning: four more than last week when I robed and vested and proceeded in a dignified fashion to the altar. But no one came. The first time I've been unable to celebrate on a Sunday. I was very sad.

Got stuck on a small wooden bridge today. But not for long.

A leech got stuck on me too, but not for long either. They are quite painless; obviously it is their stock in trade to be so, otherwise you would notice them at once. I have had too, my first real view of a snake: apparently sleeping in a tree.

Ravenshoe. March 64

On Monday I went to see a little boy in hospital. And by way of

introductory remark, asked if he remembered who I was. "You poured the water on my head" he said: which is, I suppose, a pretty adequate description of Baptism: at least in its visible aspect.

A game or so of tennis with the children. (At last Murray has hit the ball over the net six times in succession. What a triumph!) All my meals out. A couple of evenings' table tennis, and a film yesterday and the "Sundowners" tomorrow.

When I say all this, you'll realise I present a different image from the traditional Missionary. Not heroic enough, and Cecil M. de Mille would have the dickens of a job to make a dramatic film of it.

Your letter, by the way, reached me safely: despite its scanty address. "The Rev. G. Jeffery, N. Queensland, Australia." Which says something for the Post Office out here. Though not so much, I suppose, as John B.'s letter addressed to him: c/o. Innot Hot Springs, Australia. Hot Springs consists of a few corrugated iron huts and, I believe, one pub beside one of the roads we travel. And I'm not at all sure I haven't invented the pub!

On the subject of picture houses (not cinemas) here, small children are taken; on Friday and Saturday especially. A lot of what would be "X" certificates in England are seen by little children, or at least "slept through". On Friday I went with Mabel and Kevin, after having tea together. Their three children slept. Kenny, aged $1\frac{1}{2}$, and Jennifer (5) on the floor. Gregory ($2\frac{1}{2}$) on his father's lap. After, as you would imagine, some fidgeting . . .

Almost the whole town seems to turn out for these pictures.

N.B. It sounds an awful thing to say, but the only thing I can clearly remember, looking back over 6 years, about J.'s christening, was that his father smoked a cigarette in church. All the rest—meeting the family beforehand—arranging the details—explaining the service—and showing J. the font so he would not feel shy—all this, and the receiving of one little member into Christ's Church, have faded with the years compared with this one vivid, yet utterly unimportant, detail.

I suppose it is because it perplexed me at the time. Should I ask him gently to put it out? But then, this was God's home—and surely he should feel 'at home' here too, even if not to this extent? Perhaps, who knows, he was only smoking out of nervousness: because he found the whole place unfamiliar: and his wife had arranged the christening while he was at the timber yard. On the other hand, his little boy's christening was holy (I hoped) as well as homely.

As it was: all my silly secret worrying didn't matter a bit. He'd finished his cigarette, and flicked the stub neatly out of the window, before we got down to business.

St. Peter's Rectory, Collinsville. April 64.

I said goodbye to the little congregation at Ravenshoe on Sunday after Evensong. At least, due to Jimmy's guitar and Irene and Mabel, our Sunday School has gone from 3 to 30. And I've hopes that the first Aborigines ever (recollected) may soon attend. John (the R.C. padre) called to say goodbye with a parting gift of the N.E.B. How kind of him. I shall miss our journeys together to teach at Mt. Garnet, and our games of tennis at the school. The local rail car (small bus) called for me,

and after I had managed to fasten my bulging case ('Port' in Australian) it took me to Innisfail, through the Rain Forest: with its cicadas going 'cicada cicada' all the time: by rubbing their legs together.

The train to Collinsville was a casual affair. Going too far

33

and then going back to drop an old lady at her stop.

We stopped for tea at one station, served by a little girl who had to be helped with the change. The earlier journey to Bowen I spent with the Driver, being shown how it worked. A loud hoot told the distant barmaid further up the line it was time to

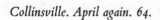

put the kettle on high, and make the tea. Dr. Beeching would hardly approve this slap-happy arrangement.

Collinsville. April again. 64.

The Rectory here is spacious, looks like this, and having little furniture and no carpets is easy to clean (an hour once a week should be enough).

I start in earnest tomorrow with lessons at school. How I dread them! Flo and Tib my neighbours are very kind. As I have 2 priests staying for the moment, Flo offered me the use of her closet if ours overflowed!

P.S. Have started scything our Rectory grass which is nearer a jungle than a garden. I drank fourteen glasses of cordial in one scything session.

Collinsville. April '64

On Saturday the 25th, Anzac Day, I gave the address and prayer at the Dawn Service. 4.28 a.m.: to commemorate the Australian and N.Z. troops killed at the Dawn attack on Gallipoli. I stood on the balcony to speak, and in the dim twilight 30 or so men stood to attention, their white shirts visible under the electric light. One or two of them seemed to be in pain, to be standing

at an angle, with heads hanging down. The reason for this appeared afterwards, when they came inside to have some drinks, already smelling strongly of the same. Many had glazed looks, and one gentleman in particular was incoherent, though very voluble.

It was he who at the Anzac luncheon (13 hours later) was still so influenced that, when asked to toast the fallen comrades, he made a speech, and sat down without having done so. He also twice said "the day we celebrate" to the obvious annoyance of the Chairman beside me who kept muttering "commemorate! commemorate!" But celebrate did indeed seem the apter description.

The waiters tottered about, and when the Chairman stood up, one promptly flopped down in his chair and had a talk with me. It was only with the greatest difficulty that we could get him out of it.

But the Chairman himself, fortified but not domineered by the Demon Drink, carried on through N. Anthem, toasts, counter toasts, appeals to small children to keep quiet, and much else, until, at about 2.30 p.m. I slipped quietly from the Hall.

I played my first game of golf last Saturday. It was a joint effort
of the Golf and Tennis Clubs. And if you are puzzled as to the
workings of this, I must explain that each golfer "adopted" a
tennis player: so that each of us, experienced and utterly ignorant,
played alternate strokes. I drew Lenny: or rather, I should say,
poor Lenny 'drew' me. And so we started off
together, at the first hole: Lenny showing me how
to hold the racket (I mean 'club') and how to try and
hit the ball. After various misses I eventually got
going: and whenever the ball went in the right
direction, Lenny shouted
out "a bottler. A
real bottler!"
(which I took to
be high praise).

Around four we knocked off for refreshments: and I was
"shouted" a couple of glasses of beer. Not the first Australian
beer I'd tasted, for Keith at the pub gives me a glass with my
free Friday supper (how generous they are)—and probably only
two thirds of a pint in all. But it was enough to put me off my
game—or perhaps it was just the end of my beginner's luck?
Anyway, poor Lenny never had occasion to shout "bottler"

again. One ball I hit right out of the golf course into the Australian bush—and it has never been found to this day. Another I directed right—but it hit a tree—and bounded back nearly decapitating me. But this, I maintained, was bad luck:

as there were not many trees about: and I just happened to hit the only one there. Afterwards, there was a supper, but Rod (he was playing too) and I didn't stay. Off back to our respective Rectories, to complete tomorrow's sermon.

Collinsville. May 64

It is raining. And those words, while boring and repetitious to you, are golden here. I even stopped my sermon preparation to stand and gaze thankfully out of the window. Just as, at Hot Springs (near R'hoe), the little Aborigine children had run out of their corrugated iron huts to stand happily in the rain, holding out their hands to catch it . . .

Seeing that I often return with gifts from visiting, I am well-stocked with food. For instance: one Mr. P., whose walls were littered with pictures of Lenin, Trotsky, Russian children, astronauts etc. gave me a box of vegetables. I staggered back to the Rectory to find a huge carton of groceries, some few pounds' worth. Scones on the fridge, tomatoes inside, and so the tale continues.

While I think of it could you send my black sketching pen, also appropriate cuttings of Somerset's progress (just the final results, with comments of each Match)? I do not mind missing local wars, political upheavals, scandals etc. But I draw the line at cricket.

Russell, the little boy opposite, came in at "smoko time" today. I had just squeezed the juice out of one solitary and precious grapefruit and was about to drink it when he appeared. Duty bound, I poured half into a glass for him: and sweetened it with sugar. He sipped it cautiously: then seemingly satisfied, gulped it back all in one go, and licked his lips. Angling for a bit of praise. I asked him: "Did you like it, Russell?" He looked back in that confidential way children have, and replied, "It was awful!"

Thank you, as ever, for your nice letters. They take five days to arrive, but of that two days at least are spent trundling up the East Coast of Australia. Our Post Box is at the front gate, and is really a tin box with a door . . . which the Post boy fills, when I'm lucky, between 12 and 3 p.m. Then off he goes, after blowing his whistle.

Jack doesn't even need the whistle. He goes by the tyre marks, or their absence, on his dusty pavement outside.

C'ville. May 11. 64

One of our little boys, Ronnie, has been missing 24 hours in the bush. The mines are closed down, men on horseback, car, foot, even plane, were out all night and day. All the other clergy are away (at Synod in Charters Towers) so I'm waiting here to see what use I can be. In fact, I was to have 3 funerals. One was at

Proserpine, 100 miles or so away. The Rector's wife must have heard I was nearby, and contacted me: her own husband being already on the road to Charters Towers, and impossible to stop. I went to Proserpine first: stopping at the edge of Collinsville to ask our younger policeman Brian (on horseback) if I could be of any use: and saying I would in any case be back quite soon. He just smiled, and asked me to keep a look out along the hills: but of course, there were far better searchers than me about.

I arrived at Proserpine in good time for the Service: and as I washed in the vestry beforehand, a little gecko surprised me by popping his head out of the plug hole to see what was going on.

Later that evening, I had two phone calls. One was from Bowen's churchwarden, 50 miles away and near Collinsville. An old lady had died, and Wally being away like everyone else, Henry the warden asked if I could come over: which of course I could. I was only sorry that in both these Services I had been unable to visit the families beforehand. Its so much better if they have their own Rector: or at least someone who's made an attempt to know them beforehand. Even so, the families (and the one at Bowen was very small) seemed grateful that I was there. Alas . . . it is a hot country: and funerals have to be taken quickly, soon after death: otherwise decay sets in.

The other phone call was from Collinsville: confirming what I had heard on the local news: that little R's body had been found. So I went back home, to see R's family once again. And the next day I buried him. First the service in Church. Then the little procession of hearse and cars going slowly through the silent main street (it is only short: and the shops on each side are very quiet). Then gathering speed a little as we leave the town and have about a mile to go before we turn left, into apparently empty bush: but really, after a hundred yards or so of dusty track, into the Cemetery.

It is a lonely place. Well out of sight, and out of town. Though not nearly so lonely as those outback gravestones one

comes across, some of them ornate and elaborately carved, but covered with undergrowth: commemorating some family, who'd lived in this or that remote cattle station years before.

Even in Collinsville there are not many funerals. Where in Southampton I once had four on one day, here in all we have about 8 or 9 a year of which perhaps I take 4 or 5. So that Jack's huge black hearse, which dates from nineteen thirty something, is allowed to go on the roads, untaxed, by the local police. In the old days, I'm told, the Miners would walk before the hearse when one of their own was buried: at least through the main street. But that was before my time . . . and I go on hearsay.

Now, at any rate, we have stopped. R.'s family, a few friends and I, are around the graveside. And I have no need to remember our Principal's remark in Theological College. "Always remember. It may be your 300th wedding, but it is their only wedding. It may be your 200th funeral: but it is R's only funeral . . ." It is, in fact, one of the very few remarks I remember at all from College days and I suppose one remembers it because it is so obvious: and you would (one hopes) have acted on it anyway.

Afterwards, just a little time with R's family. Then, my sad duties done, I drove 200 miles to C. Towers: arriving at 11.30 p.m. It was very dark, I'd never been there before and I had difficulty in finding my way to bed.

Collinsville. May 25. 64.

Last week I visited the Foxes: church folk, some 30 miles out on a cattle station. Jennifer, aged 9, stuck to me like a leech: even standing beside me while I cleaned my teeth.

43

She and I spent some time by the banks of the river searching for 'their' crocodile. Later, from high up on the opposite bank, we did just see him. But we must have breathed deeply, or disturbed a blade of grass, because he at once disappeared. And we were a good 3 or 4 hundred yards away it seemed. How on earth anyone gets close enough to be eaten by one remains a complete mystery: they seem so nervous. But I suppose they are braver if you happen to meet in the water!

Another homestead had its own swimming pool and zoo: including a camel caught in the West, friendly dingoes, wallabies, kangaroos, galahs. This station, our biggest, employs some hundred men: so totals in all something over 200 people: a small village.

Collinsville. June 64.

Six months ago that I landed in Brisbane.

Things, like things in England, follow one another and are

44

much the same. Although the parish life as 'Rector' seems rather 'bits and piecey'. It is not easy to concentrate and give yourself wholly to a sermon, for instance: when you have to choose hymns, take choir practice, clean church, polish the brasses, paint pews, measure broken windows, run working-bees on the church grounds. There are so many etceteras that the Services and visiting are from time to time submerged. I am even judging a fancy dress show on Saturday!

Collinsville. June 17. 64.

We have had our first Confirmation a week ago. I went down to Bowen to collect the new car—a Volkswagon: also the Bishop. The old Landrover was too old, and despite 4-wheel drive (which is supposed to get you out of bogs and muddy creeks), the Brotherhood felt that Collinsville hadn't enough bogs and muddy creeks to warrant it. Henry made me hold out for £600 on the old car: which I was loathe to do, not being a bargainer. But if Ray's garage makes a loss on it, I am secretly determined to pay him back the difference.

It is so difficult to fix on a fair price, it seems, in the car industry. Bob's garage said the Landrover was worth only £400!

In a way, I was sad to see her go. She had 'Mary Kathleen'

written on her side doors: which does not stand for the previous brother's girl friend. Though I suppose it does stand for somebody's girl friend, long long ago. As Mary Kathleen was the town John served: but which is now completely disbanded, because the mining of . . . (I forget what) . . . is all cleared up and finished. His old parishioners are as far away, some of them, as South Australia. And he stayed with one or two of them on the way home.

We had six Confirmation candidates: whom John had begun to prepare in his few weeks here. And 53 at the service, with a lovely meal to follow. But poor Grosvenor made an awful show at cutting the Confirmation Cake! Rod, our Methodist Minister, came along too.

Collinsville. June 25. 64.

After 6 weeks of no films (pronounced FIL-AMS here) I have seen two in a week. One with Roderick, the Methodist Minister (who has frequent meals here, and is a frequent opponent or partner in tennis). The second, after E'song, on Sunday was called "Scream of Fear". All about dead bodies appearing, and Bob and Ethel who took me in one case smoked furiously and in the other hid her head.

When I returned to the Rectory two eyes stared at me in the

46

darkness from my bed. I had the shock of my life. It was, of course, a cat: of whom a great variety seem to walk in and out of the house as they please. But then, the doors (except during rainstorms) are always open.

Sorry to nag, but where are Somerset in the Championship Table?

Collinsville 1964.

The visiting continues much as usual. At first people were shy: and even one or two of our church folk seemed not quite to know why on earth, or in heaven, I had called. When in fact I

47

had simply called to see them, without any ulterior motive whatsoever.

Have started also more general visiting; families of children who are put down as 'C. of E.' for instance, at school. Mrs. Baker said to me one Sunday lunch, after I had been here 3 weeks, 'Of course, Brother: you get on marvellous well with the people'. I was rather pleased to hear this, as I had not previously suspected it. But my "getting on marvellous well" turned out to be based on the rather unimpressive virtue of *not* trying to get

people to go to church (in which no doubt, I *am* a success!). But this is probably the best way of going about it . . . just being available, in case you're wanted. Anyhow, its what I do: however unheroic it sounds. And I am quite happy to be kept standing on the doorstep, or to introduce myself to Johnny's wife who peers cautiously through the slit in a window high up . . .

so that I have to
crane my neck.

But at least the children are not shy of me. (I had them jeering
at me once in Ravenshoe, I remember: perhaps because of my
beard). And they turn up, when you are visiting someone in
their road, to ask if you are coming to "my house". One little

boy, aged about 4,
climbed up on the
gate and said "Why
don't you come to
tea on Monday?":
an expression he had
evidently picked up
from his Mother.
But which discom-
fited her consider-
ably, because she did
not take up the
suggestion!

49

Florence gives me "cow's milk" in my tea. But she and Les stick to the proper powdered milk, which people used before the Milkman came.

Flo Baker tickles me rather when she gives me tea. Always remarking "Now, Brother; you take cow's milk in yours, don't you?" As if her own powdered milk were the norm; and the cows had only recently begun to break in on the market, with a new fangled form of milk, of which Florrie could not approve.

But this in fact dates from the not so distant past, when Bernie with his milk van and his cooling plant had not arrived: and powdered milk was the only sort available. Even so, I'll stick to this "cow's milk": so long as I can!

Collinsville. July 1. 64.

Feeling v. tired. Not through activity, though I've written three letters. But through Old Man River's Problem, of just keeping rolling along. School yesterday and Friday. Visiting, Thursday and Friday. Cleaning Church, Sat. So must complete, or at least begin, my sermons today. The little Bible Class goes well, but they eat an awful lot of cakes. Shall have to limit them to two each!

Collinsville. Aug. 6. 64.

Bill and I are through a round of the Men's Doubles. It happened on this wise. When as we were all three on Court, and many cars and audience parked outside, it became evident that the fourth man was not there. It later turned out he was asleep. But a 'phone call brought him along 40 minutes late. His partner was two parts "full" but the latecomer was not so inhibited, being ten parts "full". He laughed merrily, and whenever my partner hit one to him, said "the Rat".

The game commenced. I hit the 1st ball out; and one of my Sunday School children, of whom there were a great number, shouted "Who's winning, Brother?" In the event we played badly, but even so couldn't lose a single game. J, wholly inebriate, flayed wildly at every ball, and once even missed his own service.

It was all high comedy, and my neighbours said they hadn't had such a good laugh for ages.

Three sermons yesterday: one in the Methodist church, where I took service for Rod who is away. Too tired to write a normal letter, so I'll draw my first journey (120 odd miles) to Mt. Coolon. Got car full of dust.

Mrs. Boyd, house surrounded by animals. (Her husband, I'm told, drove off the edge of this; the longer road to Mt. Coolon, some years back.)

52

Tom Atto, stockman, says "Hope you do not mind Bushman's Tea". But gives me too much meat.

Then a cup of tea with Ken Maltby who lives in a caravan and grades (straightens) the roads. He was standing beside the road with a letter, which he wanted me to deliver in Coolon. But he had no need to flag me down. I'd have done so anyway, as you see so few people on these outback roads.

Only *one* place signposted. Meet three cars in three days. See kangaroos at dusk, bounding away into bushes.

Mt. Coolon. Founded by Tom Coolon who discovered gold in the thirties. Six houses here. It is a ghost town living on its memories, for the gold prospectors came and went years ago.

Six families. Some houses *not* houses, but corrugated iron huts: where wife has to get water by bucket etc.

I had my first wedding for 13 months on Saturday. A full church, as you would expect since it seats only 50 odd. I went to the Reception, and left after the bride's father, with whom I was sitting, had made his speech. Actually, he replied to a toast

before the toast was proposed, a slip which nobody minded. The Master of Ceremonies called on various members of the party for speeches and songs.

Weddings take place here (usually) around 5 p.m. so as to avoid the burden and heat of the day. Not that they do really, and salad is the invariable diet in the Anzac Hall afterwards. I was a little nervous at this wedding breakfast—in case I should be asked to make a speech. But all I had to do was say Grace, and I could manage that.

"AMEN"

I don't know whether its a good thing to be so wooden in my habits. But I seem to write out my sermons always on a Saturday evening. So I had to leave early anyhow. The festivities, I gather, went on with increasing jollity till 10 or 11 p.m.: but not quite up to Anzac Day standards! So I "tied the knot" for my first time, Australian style: as Lester put it. But at least we started in exactly the same way as you do. With a little crowd of schoolgirls and mothers mainly, waiting at least half an hour for the bride to arrive. The former looking forward, I imagine, to

their own white wedding with two bridesmaids or even three: and the latter looking back on theirs with (I hope) happiness.

Had an un-nerving experience three days later. At the Annual Meeting of the Country Women's Association the President handed me an illegible sheet of paper with the words, "I am

going to ask you to reply to this Motion". You could not have knocked me down with a feather, since Rod the Methodist Minister had warned me. So I had accepted the invitation with the proviso that I had to leave at 11 o'clock.

This good woman handed me the paper at two minutes to eleven. I said I had no idea what to say, which was true. And when asked if I would like to, said not. A little perplexed at this lack of verbosity in a quarter normally supposed to be heavily endowed, she passed the paper to Rod. This was not intended by me, and I found myself in a parlous plight. For if I did not, Rod would have to. In fact, he had a joke up his sleeve. (My mind was a blank.) And he read through the paper with his mouth full of cake (with his eyes actually, but his mouth was full at the time). This at least showed confidence. I'd hardly eaten a scrap at the Synod dinner, when asked to make a debut with my tongue (if you remember, I'd seriously thought of doing a bunk then, but I was no where near the door). Fortunately this time there was a door behind the lady President, of which I then availed myself, and drove over to Scottville school for two lessons.

After taking an old lady her Communion this afternoon, her daughter said: "What a pity you had to leave so early. If only you'd known, you could have cancelled your lessons". Yes, I replied: it was a pity.

Well! Our Lord did say "be wise as serpents" didn't he. That evening played Rod at tennis, 16-14, 3-6, so who will win the Final of the Singles is a matter of conjecture. Off to Mt. Coolon tomorrow.

People, by the way, go to bed early here: and are usually in pyjamas by 8.30. Not that that matters too much. In a hot climate pyjamas are as much clothing as my shirt and shorts. But I'd noticed this earlier in Ravenshoe: when I visited one evening a local family, and at the end complimented them on the very sensible and cool clothes they were wearing. "Oh," they said, "these are our pyjamas." I only hope I had not got them out of bed.

Collinsville. Sept 19. 64.

The visit to Mt. Coolon went off well. On Thursday I visited the old gold-mine. And saw the shape of an unfortunate kangaroo in the water a 100 or so feet below. It has deep shafts, unfenced: the old machinery rusty and forlorn: as a silent memory of old Tom Coolon who discovered the gold, but whose 'claim' was 'jumped' by two men who came after him, but went to apply for a lease before he was able.
He shot them both: then himself. But the town, though the gold mining stopped here in the thirties, is still named after him.

57

Service that night was held in the Hall, where the words "Billiard Saloon" are still faintly legible above the door. Thirty-three out of a population of forty sat in the deck chairs which adorn these buildings, and by the light of two lanterns sung some hymns; and had their first service since, I imagine, the 1930's. One lady said, bar weddings and funerals, it was the first time she had ever been to "church".

For those who knelt, newspapers were used as hassocks. But it was darker than I am able to put in these little sketches.

I spent the night in the hotel, and gave "religious instruction" to all the school children before christening eight of Dorrie's children, again in the hotel, the following morning. Jack the saddler, who was to his surprise a "godfather" said, "that's the first time that's ever happened in Mount Coolon".

In a sense the set-up was almost "old world". For nearly all the "town" came to church: bar one family whose Mother was deterred by the dark, but whose children cried because they could not go. One man baby-sat. Another was "full", and that completes the list of absentees.

Nor did it matter what denomination people were. Since 'R.C.' and 'Methodist' constituted a vague memory of baby being "done" in some distant past, by a Minister who went by that name. I had lunch at an old lady's house. Though of unstable appearance, it was as bright as Betsy Trotwood's inside. Again "old world", with table neatly set, and everything ready for me.

She sent me off with eggs, cakes, vegetables, jam, chutney, tomatoes: and I broke an oil-cap on the underneath of the V.W. on the way home. Very bumpy. Very stony.

My friend Rod beat me in the final of the Tennis: so the patients at hospital sympathised with me, instead of vice versa, during my visiting this week.

After tea at the Sverdloffs yesterday, I gave three boys a haircut each. Mr. S. had brought a pair of clippers, with adjustable heads for the alternative lengths of hair required. The cause of this is the temporary retirement of Bill Gray, the local barber: which leaves our nearest barber 60 miles away in Bowen. Boris, our church-warden, cuts my hair regularly.

But back to the boys. I cut Greg and Geoff's hair, more or less satisfactorily: but little David insisted on a hair style like mine. He was not easily deterred. And accepted with many misgivings the adult explanation that my hair on the sides had slightly receded by cause of nature. He was determined to have his cut in the same style. When I asked why, he replied "to attract the dames".

I pointed out it hadn't worked too well in my case. But even so was grateful for the thought. And when in after years, with my life apparently in ruins, a smug smile still lingers round my lips, it will be because I am thinking of you, David, and re-membering your words. And like G. K. Chesterton's donkey I will say: "Fools, I have also had my hour"!

Last week I told the story of the ten lepers at Religious Instruction in school. Little Alistair grew very concerned, looking at a rash which he had on his arm. But it was 'prickly-heat' and nothing quite as bad as he had imagined.

Aligator Hole, on the way back from Blenheim... ...on Friday.

Thursday 25th I spent Station visiting. 65 miles over monstrous roads to Blenheim. Very much a case of 'turn left at the black stump'. Visited four other stations.

Sep 29. 64

N.B. The family at Blenheim said "Do come later". But, alas, I never did. In fact, with a parish of only 2,000, it was only at the end of two years that I had visited—or tried to—every home that I knew of. And most of my parish is centred on Collinsville or Scottville. Though I suppose, geographically, the parish is nearly the size of Kent and Sussex put together.

I must make a determined effort to keep the weather out of these letters. I'm in danger of making it (like sin and justification in St. Paul's epistles) my central theme. But to be blunt, there is so much of it. And short of sitting in the fridge, there is no way of avoiding it.

Saturday for instance was 95 degrees. The day sixty-two children had awaited with glee. And approx. thirty-eight adults had awaited. I refer to the Sunday School picnic. At 10 a.m. all cars had assembled at the Rectory and led by a lorry

carrying fifteen children and one priest in the back, this convoy of some dozen cars set out, through the streets of Collins-  ville, on 'Operation Picnic'. Like some conquering invader, no doubt benevolent, we waved to the townsfolk in shop and on doorstep, and trundled on: because of the dirt roads and heavy dust, at 100 yard intervals. Three or four miles out of town a Detour notice had been turned back to front: and on its back the word 'PICNIC' was scrawled large, in white chalk.

Another three miles and we came down a hill into what in England we would call a glade. A little grass, and some muddy water, strange to say. And an improvised tent, made up by the men, earlier that day.

Here we carried later three huge milk churns, full of iced cordial. Here the ladies in elegant hats served food to the children, and chatted of this and sometimes of that. Here they bandaged Wesley Verevis when he fell down and cut his arm. We played various games: Hide & Seek: Chasing each other: and even cricket. I had the greatest difficulty in getting this organised. And, sportingly I thought, allowed Robert's team to bat first. They made thirty-five; and we were twenty-one for ten when I at last had my chance and went in to bat. At this juncture some fool of a child shouted "ICE CREAM" from way down in the valley; and in less than two seconds I, the Organiser, Umpire, Priest and brother, was standing in a deserted piece of Australian bush.

Actually, I exaggerate, for Lynette waited. But all the others tore down the hill, and when Wesley fell, jumped over him in their mad scramble for the promised land.

The other notable event of last week was Mrs. Tindale's sitting on my hat. Admittedly it is a thing of straw, as Luther said of the Epistle of S. James. Also, full of holes. But that was no reason to sit on it, and to remain unconsciously impressing it, for some minutes, while I was wondering where it was. At length I saw its rim peeping out from beneath her, and had to say to her as in the films: "Excuse me, Dorrie, M'am, but I think you are sitting on my hat".

This afternoon we have tennis classes. Each child brings 6d.: and in turn they bring cordial. There are between twenty to forty in all. So two classes are held, one on Friday, one on Sunday afternoon. It's a hot job, with the sun's rays reflecting off the tarmac. Followed of course by refreshments in the Rectory.

Met little Alistair in the High Street recently. He was having great trouble with his yo-yo, (there's a craze of them just now) and couldn't get it to crawl up the string one little bit. "It's the devil making me go wrong" he explained.

Collinsville. Oct 26. 64

This letter so far has been interrupted for one hour and a half by a lady enquiring about doctrines in the Bible. Her little girls wanted to be excused: and duly did, on my back door-step; being afraid to venture further in the dark!

The new Swimming Baths have been opened. The first day it was free for everybody. But for me the Manager very kindly makes it free every day. I go on Mondays to help look after the Scottville children: and most other days as well.

Sorry I haven't written for thirteen days. But I'm fairly un-ashamed, mainly through exhaustion. The Confirmation is over. The twenty-one candidates have all had their last individual instructions. The Bishop (of N. Queensland: not Bp. Grosvenor this time) has come and gone. He was delighted by the contrast with his last visit, when one solitary man kept him company in a congregation of four or five. Our little church was packed, and twenty or so had to stand outside: coming in only for their Communion. There were eighty-two Communicants, so that I who celebrated could not put all the breads on our paten (plate). And the Bishop who took the plate to give the children their Communion found a strong wind blowing them (the breads) on the floor.

The weather has played us up, though. Cooler, but with an inch or so of rain. I got my V.W. stuck last week, and so walked

six miles to visit an outback homestead. There I had five cups of tea: and the family drove me back to help remove my car. But some good samaritan had pulled it out for me!

The Bishop himself only just got here. And Boris, Tom and I

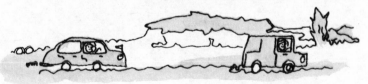

'prevented' him by Landrover for twenty miles when he had to leave. He only had one complaint: though it wasn't really a complaint at all, just a gentle comment.

"Do you know, Brother" he said. "I was in the bathroom with

both doors open when a lady walked straight through your house!" I didn't see anything strange in this myself. Indeed, when A. was very depressed and wandering about town, his wife walked in and knocked on my bathroom door. (I was in the bath: it being 11 p.m. or so). Of course, I got out and dressed.

And spent an hour or two keeping A. company as he wandered distraught through the town at night. At length I coaxed him gently to bed, and leaving his house found Rod dozing on the pavement outside. He'd heard where I was, and was waiting to see if I needed help.

Nov. 16. 1964.

A quite irrelevant post-script. But on the Day of the Confirmation I discovered a glass of beer in my post-box. I don't know who put it there, or if it was intended for the Bishop. I thought of sipping it, because it is unkind to refuse gifts, however

eccentric. Did I tell you I once found a ten shilling note stuck in my V.W. steering wheel: just where the horn in the centre leaves a little gap? And in England you have to *lock* your cars! I never discovered who put that there either.

In the case of the beer, which was in any case flat, I am ashamed to say I used it to water the plants. (Flowers is too strong a word for what appears in my garden.) This still left me with one of the pub's glasses: which I returned, somewhat shamefacedly, when I was next that way.

Collinsville. Dec 4 64

Just a year since I bought post-cards from Middle-Eastern gentlemen in Beirut, India, and Hong Kong: and wondered whether they would ever reach you. . . .

The Mines will close soon, and two thirds of Collinsville will go on holiday. Christmas here is not centred on the home: but an occasion for three weeks holiday. Shades of the old days when a special 'Mine' train took all the Miners and their families off to the coast. Both Mines, needless to say, will be shut down, and helmets are left aside. . . .

Religious Instruction, by the way, has been less of an ordeal than I imagined: and is popular with the children. "Make sure

you come tomorrow", Gwen and her little friends shout out to me.

And on one occasion when I missed class, a small boy came round to see why I had not been there. As if to say "Well, I quite understand . . . but hope to see you in your normal place next time". A nice reversal of the usually imagined relationship between pastor and erring members of his flock.

But I don't, in fact, tend to visit this way at all. Rather, to welcome those who *have* been: than to reprove gently those who have not. I did, just once, break this custom recently: when I visited our more or less regulars, and asked if they could try and come every Sunday to Communion: so that we'd all be together once a week.

Little Christine, whose granny sat on my hat, said to me "Why don't you rouse on them, Brother? Why don't you put it over the news. Have a photo of yourself with a notice 'Please Come to Church' . . ." But I never did.

Collinsville. Dec 23 64

Have taken Rod out to Mt. Coolon, on my usual visit. Carols in "church", then drinks for all on the hotel lawn. Young Colin killed a goanna. Seven miles out Rod remembered a parcel, which added fourteen miles to the journey. Also, he seems afraid of my driving: holding furiously to the side of the car whenever we go round corners! Add to this a temperature of 105 degrees in the shade and 110 or 120 in the sun, and you'll understand we had a warm journey.

Since then, the battle has been chiefly to do with our Carol singing. Our joint choir from the three churches has practised twice. The children, who are to mime the scenes, have practised once. I have planned a 'service' of 9 lessons and carols, with short lessons and comments to piece it together. "Bless this house" I have re-edited "Bless this town". Organists, guitarists, electricians, chair suppliers, lorry drivers are all ready. An Invitation in every letter box. Ten posters will line the shop windows, and one in each pub.

In my dreams it will be like Oberammergau. But Boris tells me there are only 600 (out of 2,000) left in town!

P.S.

Rod insisted that I close the car windows for some of the journey to keep the heat OUT. I had never heard of this before and told him so. But he was quite adamant. Even so, I managed to wangle mine open for most of the time.

Collinsville. Dec 31. 64.

Have been having trouble with cows and horses, rummaging about beneath the Rectory at night. Last night it was the horses. I had fixed up a piece of wire across our vacant gate-posts: which was intended to stop them getting in. In the event it stopped them getting out. For they entered by my little back gate, via someone else's garden. Tonight I should be quite secure. Though you never want to count your chickens round here. . . .

The Carol Singing started badly. At 6.30 p.m., when we were scheduled to start, the grounds were, except for two old ladies sitting patiently on a vast row of benches, entirely empty.

To make matters worse, it was too light to show the slides on the screen. We waited till 7, and then, with the light fading, we began. The best thing till then had been the procession of children, shepherds, kings, Mary, Joseph, and all, coming from

the Rectory and into the grounds. Various things went wrong. The carols on the screen were hardly legible. The spot light on the children's Mime was erratically applied by a boy on the lorry.

But I suppose these mishaps were bound to occur: or if not these, then other mishaps. By 8 o'clock when we closed down, as it were, there must have been a good 300 of us . . . sitting, standing, in cars, on the fence, and standing in the balconies of the pub beyond.

Last night Bernie, the Milkman, and I were discussing the possibilities of a similar thing for Easter. He is our chief singer, and all confidence now where he had once been very doubtful and unsure. . . .

So 'normal duties' return to Collinsville. And I go to the Hospital. And lizards run around the stumps which support the Rectory. And, every so often, a mango falls with a sickening thud on the roof; or with a gentler sound, like a bomb, on the ground. Suddenly it rains, and the parrots (who come each year to eat my mangoes) set up a chatter. And I, who have half an hour before lunch with Jack and Winifred, send my fond love and greetings as you enter 1965.

73

Stanley and Uncle
Stephen
after cake
and cordial
on Lent 1.

They come with the
parrots in December, to help me eat my
mangoes. They prefer this to
Sunday School.

P.S.

Our Ladies Guild have been very busy as well. Delivering a little greeting (signed by me) to every home: letting people know the times of Christmas Service, should they want to come: but, more important, simply taking good wishes. I hope it told the 700 or so left in town that we loved them. Certainly, it seemed to succeed in *not* bringing any new sheep back to the fold! Only Zenon came in, who had not been before, to our Midnight Mass. And that I think was partly by accident. As Boris, coming into church from Scottville, stopped to give Zenon a lift: and brought him into church with him. I don't know if Zenon wanted to come or not!

Collinsville. 65

The children have developed a funny habit here of adding the word 'but' to the end of a sentence. For instance they'll say "It's a nice day, but" or "The swimming pool closes at ten, but". It may be an Australian custom, but I'm 99.9 per cent sure it isn't; because Mrs. Fletcher (over from the church) has been complaining to me of Ronnie's stupid habit of saying "but", "which he's picked up from the kids at school". Ironically, it's spread to the grown-ups as well. Mrs. Fletcher complained a month or so back: and yet in conversation with me yesterday said "Ronnie's doing well at school, but". I suppose it just comes naturally, to a little village living, as we do, at the end of the line.

There are other traces of nice twists and varieties in language, as well. Les often speaks of the plastic children, and how we should help them. Also, at P.C.C.s, he has said he did not want to "steal my plunder". Best of all, he urges me forward, saying "we mustn't rest on our morals". Not that I have many morals to rest on, but!

Collinsville. Jan 10. '65.

Rod has left. The Methodist Ministers spend a year here usually, before completing their studies and being ordained. A year in the field, so to speak. So perhaps Rod is technically not yet a Minister, though of course he does minister, if you see what I mean!

Anyway little Douggie and I have collected about £9 so far, by visiting about eighteen non-churchgoing Methodist families. We have enough to fill the new Minister's fridge: and Don and Ruth and I (to a lesser extent) have been repainting and redecorating his bedroom . . . and oh yes, we've got him an arm chair.

76

Once more, as you see, from the Tableland. And oh, so cool! Only in the seventies. We've had two days in retreat, and two in Chapter. While you in England have been mourning Sir Winston we have followed as best we can. The flags here, and at the little convent school, and in R'hoe's main street, are all at half mast.

Some of the brothers, Derek and John among them, have finished their year's probation (postulancy is, I suppose, the better word:) and have accepted, and been accepted, for the next four years. Here they are, having their red girdles wound round and round. . . .

The rules are not too difficult, I suppose. To remain unmarried, to live on £1 a week: and to go where you are sent. But as all your working and living expenses are paid generously, this is no hardship (unless you smoke). And you are only sent by mutual agreement as to where is best. Also oh yes—you say a prayer for all the other brothers once a day. Doesn't sound too hard, does it? At least, I don't find them so (though I'm only an Associate): just as easy as keeping the 10 Commandments. Of which Mark Twain could well have said, though I am afraid he didn't, "I have no difficulty in keeping them at all. In fact, I keep them frequently."

Our trains are becoming less frequent, with the Mt. Isa strike: and consequently my two copies of 'Punch' arrived close together. For these I thank you very much. But I must confess, I failed to understand the political cartoon in one of them. Distance is at length beginning to tell. And I am joining the ranks of those old men at the Atheneum, to whom 'Punch' is not as good as it used to be`. . . like sherry, teenagers, buildings, films, etc. . . .

I returned half an hour ago from Bernie's, where we've been practising hymns for our Passion Play. The writing of it is all

done, and by twisting people's arms have managed to collect some fifteen to twenty colleagues. Both other Ministers, and their flocks, are involved. But it's been a battle. Seven of us met to discuss the possibility (3 clergy and 4 laymen!). Decided to invite 100 likely candidates as a start, and hired a Hall for the purpose. Only six turned up. Still, the fight goes on. . . .

Have been having the most awful difficulty finding men for our Play. Only three of us at Bernie's yesterday. And one of them (Bernie) has to conduct the choir: Adrian, the Centurion, came. And I, who play the Devil. I know we'll have to change parts a bit—but even so we must have twelve disciples (not to mention

78

one Other) for a kick off! Still, we had a few women to sing the hymn parts. So they seem more faithful than us men (as of course they were on the original Friday).

Greg nearly came, as he promised to. But didn't. "He's in the Shower," his Mother said, so I ran off to drag him out. He came later, but says he'll be away at Easter. Getting desperate,  is dear old Greg: I think he'd even get married and be away on honeymoon, if he could find no other way. Still, I won't press him too hard: only persist gently for a week or two!

But there are little signs of progress, and the coming of dawn. The Convent Sisters are praying for our success. And Jenny from Myuna is trying to persuade Daddy and Gan Gan (Grandad) to join in.

Collinsville. March 3 '65

Have just been to visit little Carol T. in hospital. An affectionate little child, probably through home in-security. She put her face up to be kissed, when I had to leave . . . An unusual custom, even in this informal land. But there's no saying, it might catch on. . . .

79

On Sunday Mari ($14\frac{1}{2}$) leaves. So we are giving her a party, after church. (As we do, whenever one of our flock leaves for pastures new.) Mari had only just plucked up courage to become our regular 'other' organist. But work is scarce, with this Mt. Isa strike. So her family have had to move south. Little Ronnie was my first server.

I am still recruiting for our Passion Play. Saw a young man in the pictures recently with a beard. Likely candidate, I thought. But though he turned out not to be, he led me to another "disciple". "If you go up the steps of the bottom hotel," he said, "turn right along the balcony and go right to the end: inside the door on your left you'll find a geologist called Ian, up from the South. He'll be on his bed, reading James Bond." I did as he commanded. Turned right, went to the end of the balcony, knocked on the last door. "Come in" said Ian: and put down his copy of James Bond! How I wish all people were as predictable. . . .

Collinsville. Mar 20 '65

The rains have gone, which nearly stopped our visit to see the Archbishop in Townsville. Even so, one third of the priests couldn't make it. I stayed (free) with Mrs. F. at the Newmarket: she who bought me a meat pastie on my first visit to C'ville (remember?). But I shall not need to stay there again. For I met Ken and Delma outside the Cathedral (Kenneth was Methodist Minister up on the Tableland, and I visited him once when he was sick). And they insist I stay with them during our Synod in June.

Last Sunday, another visit from the Beetles (spelt with two e's). Little black bugs which come by the hundred and oblige me to turn out the lights during Sermon time. This ecclesiastical practice puzzled our immediate neighbour, who told his wife. "I don't know what they do in the Church of England. First Brother comes down with two lighted candles. Then the lights go out. . . ." Tommy's a Presbyterian, so it must be doubly puzzling!

Been to Mt. Coolon again. After service, Jack, in his cups at the bar, told me he wanted to go to church; but was afraid because none of the other men went. In fact, we'd had a couple of cars drive in from nearby stations, which was nice. J. then divulged his family tree. Half were Anglican, half R.C. of

whom the latter were distinguished by their refusal to attend non R.C. services. He laboured this point with some venom against Fay Maltby, who was trying to encourage him to come. "What religion are you?" he asked her. 'R.C.' she replied. At which J. smiled wanly as if in misunderstanding, and continued

to . . . but here I will stop, as he eventually did, when we persuaded him to eat some stew.

It is very silent here in the bush. Grace tells me that on a quiet night, and what night in Mt. Coolon isn't quiet, she can hear a car from twenty miles away.

Going over to 'Church' in Mt. Coolon. Little pinpricks of light (in case of snakes) converging from 5 or 6 directions.

And the hum of a motor car, and its lights through the distant bush far away, when we have visitors. A shaky little table serves as altar. . . . And afterwards, at half past 8, Douggie and Pam fight over who is to put out the candles: and then, just as they came, so they fade away: little pinpricks of light getting smaller and smaller in the Australian bush.

P.S. At a week day Communion recently there was only Maureen, newly confirmed, and myself. The heat affected poor Maureen who felt faint: so I helped her lie down in the sanctuary, with a cushion beneath her head. I suggested she said 'Amen'

82

or joined in what parts of the Service she wanted to . . . then leant down to give her her Communion, holding her head gently with my free hand. She rested a little still in the sanctuary, after the Service was over. Then I got out the car, and took her home. She was quite all right later. It's, as I said, this heat.

Little Russell continues to pop in and out regularly. Yesterday

we had arranged to swim at 2.30 p.m. He arrived at 8, when I was having breakfast, already in togs. I couldn't go then, having to visit Weetalabah, Havilah and some outlying stations. When, later, I return from these visits, I find he's gone without me.

Collinsville. April 14 '65

Bishop Miles (our one episcopal brother) is staying here over Easter. And I've arranged meals out, and visiting all the faithful, for him. But he's keeping my pulpit warm for two Sundays, which gives me grace for the Passion Play.

Bishop Grosvenor, or 'Uncle Grosvenor' as the Foxes call him, has a unique way of getting on with children. Instead of trying to know them all by name, which is for him in any case impossible, he just uses any name that comes into his head. For instance, he calls Jennifer "Hepsibah": and Wesley Verevis "Edward": (or is it "George"?) These children, of course, he

knows. But any child he meets is liable to be greeted as "Elizabeth" or "Frederick" or "Selina": and they seem to like it very much. As if he had chosen a name especially for them. (He does, of course, get the sex right!)

83

Also, I am afraid to say, he was a bit critical of my driving. I collected him from Bowen, where we had a meal with Henry and Mary. Then I took him by road to Collinsville. On the way we hit a stone: or at least a large stone struck the underneath of my V.W., upon which Grosvenor gave a great start and said: "You are as bad as Brother Basil. If there is a stone or boulder anywhere in sight, he manages to hit it."

I thought this was a bit hard. Partly because the road is made up of rocks and stones and boulders anyway. And its a question usually of which stones to go for. But more particularly, because I had spent some months with Brother Basil. And thought I had found in him a driver more erratic than myself. He is what you would call a "Bush Christian": relying on the Lord for help. And driving constantly on the centre, or occasionally the right hand side of the road. Of course Basil is a dear: and one hesitates to comment on this sort of driver. Because almost invariably they prove you wrong by escaping accident. While the rest of us, who think we are better, end up upside down in some ditch. You know, like Grandad. He always, I remember you telling me, drove on the right hand side of the road: and yet only had one accident, when he bumped into a lorry: and that was the other person's fault.

Basil is a bit like that. On one occasion he drove John, my predecessor (for a few weeks) here, and I to "Little Milly" for a bathe. As he backed out of the Rectory, I warned him to stop: so one small boy on a bicycle did not get run over. Thereupon, Basil promptly zoomed out of our little side road, forcing Neville and his Ravenshoe Bus onto the grass verge on the other side. Brother John seemed genuinely terrified. He made the sign of the cross in great agitation (and haste): which I took

to be, well . . . not irreverent of course, but not quite in earnest either. But apparently he was: because after our swim, he got the car-keys from Basil and insisted on driving back. I myself hadn't felt nervous at all. Not certainly through courage. More likely, through usage! And dear Basil took it all in good part: utterly unresentful at any suggestion of aspersion on his driving. And as oblivious of the local bus, as he had been of the bicycle!

Yesterday, we had two dress-rehearsals for our play, the first time everyone was there for practice.

Fr. Ryan is helping to arrange our stage; and is printing some 300 copies of the hymns for our audience/congregation. He is hoping for the best.

On Sunday we went to the aerodrome for an open air practice. Our twelve cars went in convoy, a noble procession. Tomorrow we take round a lorry occupied by Roman soldiers and disciples:

this is a tour of C'ville and Scottville, advertising by loud speaker "Good Friday 8 p.m. Gordon's Allotment". You cannot say we are not trying.

Our Milkman is Pilate. And the Cafe owner, Judas. I, as Narrator and Compère, am the Devil. Having had to fight so hard and been told all along that it was impossible, Tom yesterday had to comfort me. "It'll be all right, Brother, just you see".

By the by, if I ever say I've been visiting from 9 a.m. to 5 p.m. as sometimes, but not often, happens: please do not worry. I get my meals all right. People invariably press you to stay to lunch, if one o'clock is even remotely in sight.

Collinsville. April 22 '65

Well, it's all over. And the Passion Play was all I wanted it to be. Some Miners from the Scottville Mine put up a huge stage: our churchwarden arranged fluorescent lighting round the ground. After so great a struggle to get actors, and to get them to practices (they didn't all turn up together till a week ago) it went marvellously well. They spoke up, though in truth there was not much speaking. And the choir sang well. The audience/congregation numbered about 900. It looked a little like this. . . .

86

I hope now to do a Christmas Play with hymns. I wonder we do not do it in England more. One or two little children were afraid of me as the Devil. And Billy, aged two, when I put on my mask shouted "Where's Brother Jeffery gone?"

N.B. Looking back, again over the years, perhaps my most vivid memory is the first glimpse I ever had of the stage. I'd been so busy with this and that, beforehand by day, that though I'd noticed the stage going up, I had not really taken it in. Not, that is, until I had finished my work: and went, in the dark and comparative cool of the evening, to see the stage which was supported on barrels, by the way. It was, in a sense, the nearest I've ever been to a feeling of humility.

So often, as a parson, you work with intangibles: and do not see anything concrete or physical that you can get hold of and say 'this I have done. This I have achieved.' Not of course that I'd raised a

87

finger (well, perhaps one or two) to build this! Ron and Greg, Boris and the Scottville Miners had done it all. But at least it was something tangible: something I could feel and get hold of, and say: 'This is something thats happened because under God of me'. It hadn't really. But I felt so grateful that I drove straight out to Scottville to say thank you to Boris. But Lynne came to the door and said he was asleep.

Perhaps it was the same sort of feeling young Ian had at a later play (he was one of our original disciples, and stuck with us right through). He was sitting on the stage the evening before, with a friend from school. And looking up at the stage, he said: 'People say Collinsville's a pretty poor sort of place; but we can't be that bad if we do this sort of thing'.

Another memory comes back. At the end of the first play, a group of Methodists gathered round the piano. And quite oblivious of the crowd melting away, burst into song. Can you say 'burst into hymn'? That's what it was anyway. An utterly spontaneous act: with all the agonies and difficulties of putting on the play completely forgotten.

88

Did I tell you of my first attempt to attend a Meeting of our Alcoholics Anonymous? Its a good society: and I like very much their saying to each other "Now you are one day old. Now you are two days old. Now you are three. . ."; as one of

" NOW YOU ARE ONE DAY OLD "

their members manages with help to go one, two, three, days without a drink. I have one or two friends who belong, and I was grateful when they asked me to come. Not that I felt I could do much. In such a hot and thirsty land the pub is usually the first port of call after a tiring day at the mine: and it must be terribly difficult to keep out. Anyway. Back to the Meeting. "It's at 8 p.m." my friends said, "in the Convent School". So at 8 p.m. prompt I duly turned up. To my surprise the Meeting was already in progress, which should perhaps have warned me. Because 8 p.m. in Collinsville usually means sometime around 8.30. Anyway Fr. Arthur Ryan (R.C.), who appeared to be "in the chair" said "Oh, come on in. I'm afraid we're on some boring business at the moment." They were. Bazaars, fetes, and the like. I knew all the people there, and assumed that they would get on to Alcoholism in due course.

It transpired later that the Meeting was not A.A. at all: but a Meeting of the R. Catholic's P.C.C. or its equivalent. And my name "The Rev. Brother G. Jeffery" appeared on the Minutes as a Guest for the night.

It says something for inter-church relations here that no-one was in the slightest surprised that I should be there. They stood as I entered and smiled a welcome. And when I said "I'll just sit down quietly and listen" everyone assumed it was the most natural thing in the world. Apart from this sidelight on Christendom in Collinsville—a boring and dull thirty minutes for me. It is hard to be inspired by Bazaars.

I took a special celebration for Rae yesterday: one of our first to be confirmed, she's off to New Zealand for a year. Most of our young people have one ambition, to move south: (they cannot move north in any case): also, while you in England long for a suntan, Australian girls envy your fresh complexion. Certainly, the girls in the very outback sometimes age prematurely: and (though this is different) I took Mary with her close cropped hair and cowboy clothes in one outback settlement, for a man. But she didn't mind: only laughed.

Collinsville. May 15 '65.

I'm sorry I disappointed you with my account of this year's Anzac celebrations. But they were, I am afraid, rather tamer than last year's. So I had better fill in one or two details.

I arose at 4. And went to the Workers' Club where the Diggers, or Returned Soldiers, were established. I had a cup of coffee,

and then we marched in darkness to the Anzac Hall. We were soberer than last year, although the person in front of me walked at a slower pace than the rest of us. And those unable to make the March were carried in cars.

The Dawn Service was unremarkable, I am sorry to say. Fr. Ryan tells me he copped a few drunks at his 7 o'clock Service. One man came in and refused to take off his hat. Later he left, but his voice kept coming through the open windows. "Where's the beer?" he kept shouting in the vernacular; according to the decisions of the latest Vatican Council. He thought Jock had the beer, and came to church to find Jock.

Our Service came half an hour later. And those who came were as sober ... hic ... as myself. But one shadowy figure did emerge in the doorway during the last hymn but one, as the Communion was ending. He sat slumped in an empty seat beside the door. And afterwards thanked me profusely for my sermon, which he had fortunately missed: but, for that reason perhaps, had doubly appreciated.

Last Thursday, on the way to Bowen, I stopped at Mount Aberdeen. About 3,000 ft, it is 6 miles off the road: and $1\frac{1}{2}$ miles

from where I left the car. Gordon Thormalein, who lives at the foot, asked me to report back when (and if) I returned: otherwise he would come out and collect me. Fortified with this assurance I launched a one-man assault on the summit.

One mile of inpenetrable bush, snake-skin whose occupant had happily departed, cliffs climbed to be found in vain, prickly grass which pierced and clung to my socks, blade grass which cut my legs when I took them off (my socks I mean): these and many other obstacles reduced my effort to a 10 to 2 p.m. failure: as I ended back at Gordon's shack. Here his old parents, up from Bowen, made me a meal . . .

It's amazing how indifferent you get to the peril of snakes. At first I was afraid to put one foot in front of the other without inspecting my next step in detail. Later, you say to yourself "Oh, they'll hear me and scamper off" so you just make noises as you walk. (This is a delusion, because the deaf adder *is* deaf, and hence very dangerous: getting its other name of "death adder".) Later still, after three or four hours you remember that only *one* man—a farmer—has been bitten by a snake in well over a year and the wireless says he's getting better. Besides, the snakes are far more afraid of you than you of them: and no statistics are available for the hundreds of snakes killed by humans. I'm not defending my attitude. Just explaining how one's reasoning changes, on a hot afternoon's walk!

Did I tell you I met Dame Enid Lyons? Her Jo was P.M. back in the 1930s. 20 years older, he met her when he was an Inspector of schools, and she a little nine year old recited a poem or something for his benefit. One of their daughters is our butcher's wife: a son is in the Mine Office. I have her autograph, and when her biography comes out in September I'll buy you a copy and enclose the autograph . . .

She told me she was first conscious of Jo as a person when she was fifteen and he thirty-five: since he visited her home fairly often. When she was sixteen he fell in love with her, and they married a year later: Jo being thirty-seven, and his bride seventeen. But this is Enid's story not mine: though I find it very romantic, in an Old Testament sort of way.

The children here are wonderfully independent. Mrs. B. is in hospital, and Christine aged thirteen is in charge of the house. She cooks well, irons, and when she is away, Pauline who is younger looks after the five or so younger still.

The children all say "good-day" when you see them, and "hooray" when they leave. You don't "feel right" rather than not "feel well". And you pour out the tea by drips and drops, letting the pot heel back on its fulcrum, or whatever it is. This is to ensure strength, so that a mouse can trot across it, as you would say . . .

Synod was more interesting than last year, although just as long. Starting with Matins at 6.30 a.m., we finished debating around 11.00 p.m. I stayed with Delma and Ken Cutmore. Kenneth is a Methodist Minister in the suburbs of Townsville, and was on the Tableland as I think I told you. When I left Ken's house to see his church, fifty yards away, he said "Be sure and lock the door".

Which surprised me. My Rectory is 180 miles away: both front and back doors, as well as windows, are open. It never occurs to me to close them. Of course, if there's a storm, dear Flo from next door will run over and close it up . . .

And today? No school, which was fortunate as I overslept. I cleaned the house, scrubbed my two wooden toilets, did the weekly wash. . . .

Mount Coolon next week. Perhaps you are, today, warmer than I. I hope you are able to see a good bit of Wimbledon.

C'ville. June 30. '65

Yesterday, S. Peter's Day, we had Evensong with our usual party in the Rectory. Forty came, of whom some twenty-five were children. And now? I am in shorts again. And have taken off my jersey. My brief flirtation with long trousers is over. I've done my wash, and put it back in action: a sheet washed is always ready to go back on the bed in four or five hours.

I have swept the house, always dusty because our road is of loose and dry sandy earth, and the wind this way.

Thank you so much for your papers and 'Punch'. They come sporadically, like poetic inspiration to the Author. In fact, I had four 'Punches' on the same day recently. A little much even for my elastic sense of humour.

Collinsville. June '65.

I have just received a letter from Anthony full of woes: over Vietnam, poor Mr. Wilson, the Budget etc. But now at twenty to eight, Australian time, I hear Christine Truman has defeated Nancy Ritchie: and all is well with the world once again. With such a victory, beneath our belts, we are ready to take our place

once more in the Council of Nations . . .

We've been caught in a frightful cold snap: in which I for one had difficulty in keeping warm. The temperatures were around freezing point at nights: and I had to heat my bed with a frying pan off the electric stove . . . I closed one of my inside room's three doors (we have no heating, of course). And had no mosquito net: and the children (approaching forty eight) for tennis coaching had hot tea instead of cordial. I was almost pleased to see the mosquitoes again, for the cold had knocked them almost as lifeless as myself. At breakfast, by the way, I have hot porridge and wrap a blanket round myself to keep me warm. I suppose it's the change of temperature which makes me do this: for I never had porridge in England. By nine o'clock I need a jersey, but by ten I don't, and by mid-day we're back in the nineties again.

C'ville. July 15 65

On Saturday night I finished my sermon early. And in the remaining hour before bed-time, began to draw a cartoon or two

of Barnabas as a monk. And the creative urge kept me darting out of bed to put fresh ideas on paper: and has only now, on Thursday 12.05 a.m., finally abated: leaving on my desk some 100 or so sketches . . .

96

I have been fairly ecumenical in my interests. Sketching children at the Women's Auxiliary Party (supposedly left wing) being Fr. Ryan's guest at the R.C. Wells' Dinner, (Like these Stewardship Schemes. Ended with a Hymn played by Record Player, which I would have joined in, if I'd known the words. But no-one else seemed able to make much of it either.) and going to lunch at the Methodist garden party.

Last Saturday I had a nightmare that no-one came to church. It nearly came true. At 7.25 a.m. only two little girls stood outside. But by the end of the first hymn we had risen to twenty-two.

Choir practice tonight, if anyone turns up . . .

Bimbo, who asked for a drink on Wednesday

The Courier-Mail, Queensland's daily paper, has produced an article on our passion play entitled "Little Miracle in little Moscow". And it's been reproduced on the first page of the Townsville Bulletin. Am not too pleased at this connection of our Passion Play with politics: and have written to the C. Mail about it. Luckily, they published the letter. So any Communists here know that the Play is for all the town, irrespective of denomination or politics. And if they've any party members, I'll keep them a front seat at our Christmas one!

Spent a pleasant day in Bowen last Friday, with my friends the Darwens. Feeling tired, I phoned up to see if I could spend a day there: and arrived in time to help Henry take his local paper (which he produces) off the press. You remember what you said about the American papers: that they put in a lot of personal stuff? It's the same here. 'John on holiday with his Uncle. Gwen twenty-one last Thursday' . . . and so on.

On Friday we had a picnic lunch at Horseshoe Bay, shaped as Michael once observed, 'like a horseshoe'.

Tomorrow for my sins, I have to judge a Children's Art Competition for the show which starts on Friday.

P.S. In fact, I returned from Bowen earlier than expected. A phone call said P. was dying, so I sped back the 60 miles to spend most of the next day with him, and his family.

The last week has been a fairly Roman one. Although, the Methodist Minister being at Synod, I took a Funeral in his Church: and so redressed the balance. Arthur Ryan, twenty-five years a priest on Sunday, celebrated his Jubilee. I got our Congregation at Communion to sign a New English Bible which I then took up to the Presbytery. On Tuesday I went to the Jubilee Show or Concert, beautifully done by the Convent school-children, and spoke at the Supper which followed. (This ended with friendly songs etc, including "Why was he born so beautiful, Why was he born at all?" At which one priest said to me in disgust. "*Not* in front of his Mother!") On Wednesday, there was a lunch for the clerics, an informal lunch at separate tables, and very enjoyable too. No speeches there, although one old priest was prevailed upon to recite his masterpiece, "the old violin". 'Wait until he's had a few beers', one scheming cleric

whispered to another. But he recited it willingly enough, after the customary pretence that he was indeed unwilling; and received at the end a great accolade.

Mrs. B. has just rung me to ask me to do some posters for the annual baby show. Flo next door is very kind: washing my shirts every week, and leaving a saucer with slices of cake freshly baked or fish cakes on it, in my kitchen from time to time. The Baker never accepts money, so I get my daily bread free: and cakes from there too, or as yesterday a meat pastie for my lunch.

Please do not feel my interest has shifted entirely from God to my tummy.

The Ladies' Guild have a Meeting on at the moment. Danny, one of their children, is asleep on my bed.

On August 3, my Diary tells me, little Cheryl and I won a bar of chocolate each at the school dance. I'd gone along, after making up a little song to the tune of "Moon River", to say goodbye to a teacher called Frank . . .

On the 5th I went Bush for the day.

6th . . . Am asked to tell Jim he is dying, as requested by the doctor. Then off to Charters Towers for Retreat. At the end of which a note is given me at breakfast: "Please phone 115". So Jim has died, and I travel back 240 miles in about 250 minutes to take his funeral. Then back to Townsville (180 miles) for the Brothers' Meeting . . .

Tonight, after Evensong, a little party was put on for my birthday. And Laura (aged 4) recited "the Owl and the Pussycat" for me. She had to be helped with the words a bit: as she stumbled rather. But at the end, through sympathy on our part, received great applause. This so encouraged her that she promptly

recited it again: which was not perhaps our intention. Anyway, I'm thirty.

Talking of poetry, after my last visit to Coolon, Doug—aided by a drink or two, started reciting "Clancy of the Overflow". A touching scene, far off from anywhere, to hear the words Peter Dawson used to sing . . . in their true surroundings.

On Tuesday the Doctor and I won our first round in the tennis doubles. It afforded me great pleasure, for the Doctor's sake, since he's only played once or twice this season.

The match was sufficiently remarkable to draw some most caustic comments from onlooking cars. Our opponents, eager to brush us aside, and move one round nearer the Doubles

Trophy could hardly do a thing right. They aimed every ball at the poor doctor: who hit many out. But got a few surprise ones in, which quite discomforted them. And in the end we won 11-9, 6-4.

On Wednesday we had one of our traditional power cuts. I thought the children would stay away from their Confirmation Class; but most came, and we had our lesson by candle-light. Afterwards, by candle-light until nine, by electric till ten fifteen, I went through the Wedding Service with Raymond and Lerida. Since Raymond is deaf and dumb, this involved a longer interview than usual. And, no doubt, the Wedding itself will be

a little unusual . . . with the use of deaf and dumb language for part of the vows and promises.

My tennis coaching for this year came to an end last Saturday. With about forty children playing the first remembered Children's Championship here. Trophies were given: the children brought their own lunch, which was divided and placed on a large trestle table from which they helped themselves, feeding off it, 5,000 wise. It was very hot.

I left in the middle to take Raymond's wedding. He said 'I do' on his fingers. And nodded his assent to the rest which I read out for him. I even made a short speech at the Reception: saying with assistance GOD BLESS YOU on my fingers.

Our Christmas Play has begun again . . .

Our Mission is over. Taken by John, a friendly and happy priest from Townsville. Jocelyn, his aide de camp, took a series of children's services which were very popular. Our numbers rising from twenty-six to fifty to eighty and ninety, so that for the last two or three days I could not find a seat in church. The one time I am happy to stand.

In fact, I had to stand for one or two of the adult services as well. Mainly because of our local group "The Rovers", who gave guitar and drum support to the piano and our faltering voices. You would like to have seen Gregory, aged three, trying to twist on the rail of the back pew.

I must say, I am not normally in favour of Missions: thinking (with H. Henson is it?) that they are unnecessary in a good parish: and harmful in a bad one. Nor do I like making resolutions. But this Mission was a very friendly affair—even had a barbecue for the teenagers—and was not too religious. So when we were invited to go up for our little resolution cards, I thought I'd better show a leg. And little Neil and I went up first together.

Nearly everyone, I think, followed.

The only damage the Mission did, from my point of view, was that it helped put Colleen and I out of the Mixed Doubles. Colleen is 16, and our best girl player. Also—nice touch—she's spent a week (I think it was a week) with Frank Sedgeman's tennis-school. Which reminds me: in the Ravenshoe school, the boys there—young Keith among them—had played against another winner of Wimbledon, Ashley-Cooper. Funny, that.

I've been here less than 2 years and in both villages almost (by English standards) that I've served, I've met children who've knocked a ball about with Internationals. In 28 years of England I never met anyone at all who'd played, say, with our own Bobby Wilson. No wonder the Australians are so good. (Though of course, the weather helps!)

But back to Colleen. We played after the teenage-bar-be-cue.

It was a hectic effort, in the church grounds. With music, guitars, and a lot of jiving (in my case a form of jigging and jogging). Also, I may have done a sketch or two. There was a young Englishman there, staying overnight with the Sparkes. He said to me: "I wouldn't like your job, getting mauled all the time by the populace." I wouldn't say I was 'mauled' exactly. But when the time came for me to leave, at around 10 p.m., for the tennis: Mrs. Sparkes (another Dorothy) said to me, 'You look like death'. I felt like it. And, after joining Colleen at Scottville, played like it. I could hardly get a ball over the net: until 5 games had passed. And even when I started to, it was a bit late. Poor Colleen. She deserved better support. But was very kind about it all. (One of our first six to be confirmed. So I suppose she had to be!)

A little later David (this time) beat me in the Final of the Men's Singles. But I'd no excuse for my display then. Just nerves, when I was ahead in the Final Set. I had, it is true, done the 80/90 mile journey from Coolon. But that was no disadvantage. Once you get used to a road, with its twists and turns, creeks and gullies, but mainly emptiness and no one on the road, its quite restful. (Well, fairly restful, say.) And I'm glad for David and Colleen (his wife and strong supporter). Though

Tibby and Flo next door were sad a bit: seeing as it was my last chance.

Tomorrow I have a visit from a Television film producer: who has to make a film of Brotherhood Activities, and wishes (perhaps) to use our Christmas Play as a Finale. Which reminds me—I still have about four men to find for parts, and Mein Kampf is not yet over.

C'ville. Oct 25 65

Awakened by Peg very early to tell Harry of Mrs. J's death. We go down together to his garden, and Harry is already up. Sitting quietly in his garden with a hose, watering the grass and the plants. . . .

And I had planned to take Harry over to Townsville, on my next visit, to see her.

Collinsville. Nov 2 65

Had six or seven Thursday Islanders to Church on Sunday. They are laying a Railway Line near here: and I pop out every two or three days. Drink is a bit of a problem. But they are, which is strange, more or less Anglican to a man. Perhaps they will join our Christmas Choir: but it is early to say yet.

My car's been playing me up a bit. It broke down 38 miles from home, on its last bush visit. I am no mechanic, so I just said Evensong. And had barely finished before a car came into sight. John, the Driver, kindly took me in. And Jeff, opposite our church, said "we'd better go out at once or you'll find it pinched". So we did, Jeff, Roy and I.

Jeff's a pet. He empties our closets by night—a hard and beastly job, I should say. And I hear him sometimes around 5.30 a.m. prowling past the Rectory. (Whenever I ring the church bell, he shouts out "Say one for me, Brother".)

Bernie the Milkman is even earlier: and in my half-sleep I sometimes hear him too. As he fills my billy can, standing on the gatepost. Well soaked in some "anti-ant" mixture at the base: and if I forget, by 7 a.m. the top of my milk is filled with ants.

Our Bible class continues quite happily: though I find 12 little disciples (sometimes less, sometimes more) enough to cope with. And often seem to fight a losing battle. But in one sense it has borne fruit. As seen in the School exams on Religious Instruction (I have to set these: but wish I hadn't): when our own little flock aged 9 to 12 know far more on average than the 15 year-olds. At least they avoided Rhonda's (inevitable) definition of a centurion as 'a man a hundred years' old'. And, less expected, Ross's description of Our Lord as "a Man with a beard who has six foot tall and weares long clokes".

God, As Seen   by Ross

Bible class starts off with a shuffle and dealing of cards: like playing cards, except that I have written a duty on the back of each. "Say grace": "Help Brother wash up": "Dry up": "Say closing prayer", etc. Better than Bible reading, they like swims in the pool, and penny hikes. The latter is a walk round Collinsville with torches and a penny. Heads you turn left: Tails you turn right. And a different child spins the coin each time.

But Maree and David and co. are very artful. I read them an account from the paper recently about an American storage underground: in which baked beans, and record-players, and every adjunct of 20th century civilization was being stored up: In case of nuclear war and mass destruction. What story in the Bible did it remind them of? The answer was more or less immediate: 'Noah's Ark'. Also, once, they asked to say their own prayers: which we did in turn, sitting as usual in a sort of circle. It did not matter much that every child used roughly the same words as Susan who started: asking God to bless the Bible Class and Brother and . . . It was how the Christians started, long ago: and I was grateful for their love.

Nov 17 65

A lady from Middleton in Sussex has moved in, just opposite the school at Scottville. After lessons I popped in to see her, and remarked how close we were to her at Bognor (though not so close now). I think I got on her nerves a bit by asking too many questions. Though I didn't really summon her before a Grand Inquisition: simply enquired how she liked it, and how the family were etc. She said I was just like the Australians, wanting to know all about her. To which I think I replied, that her neighbours were only being friendly: and showing a genuine interest.

Though, perhaps, I've painted myself a bit blacker than need be. Because at the end, she seemed genuinely pleased that I had called. I'm looking forward to seeing Randal and Oenone again . . .

C'ville. Nov 29 '65

When you read this, our play will be over, and the television cameras departed. But at the moment am still in the throes of Play-birth. Today we visited both mines. And a team of four young men from Sydney took films of both. Yesterday we

trekked off to Frank the dozer-driver: miles away from anywhere in the bush! He was clearing scrub and tree and cactus, and was filmed from many angles.

As was Tony (Joseph) in the Bank, and Norma (Mary) playing at School. Frank is one of the Wise Men. Les, my Churchwarden, was tickled pink to be filmed as he gave them petrol . . .

My last visit to Coolon was none too successful. I skidded, went up a bank, and could not get the car off. I drank my water, and ate one of two of the mangoes I had brought over for Pamela.

Then I walked for two hours, hoping to reach a lone tree-cutter I'd waved to earlier. The flies settled like a blanket on the back of my shirt and hat (not happily on my face) I suppose

109

because of the draught. I failed to see anyone, so after eight miles or so retraced my steps to be back before dark. Had a little supper, prepared to sleep . . . but then headlights as I began to doze. The teacher and policeman from Coolon had arrived to drag me off with chains, and so . . . eventually, to bed.

In fact, I had been nearer help than I'd known. Doug, who drove in from town the following day, said he noticed my footsteps in the dust. "Pity you didn't go 100 yards further", he said. "There was a tree-feller round the next bend"!

Melbourne. c/o My friend Randal. Dec 9 65

The Play is over, and I'm in Melbourne which is roughly the text and message of this December Epistle. Had felt rather uncertain about the Play, and had been feeling the weight of indifference which we were trying to shift. And, no doubt, the television cameras, with their insistence on perfection, and 'time and time again', in everything they did, made a tiring business even more tiring. Certainly at the end, I felt utterly washed out. Completely flat, though not through depression so much as reaction.

Anyhow, to action. We did not get the 1500 I dreamed of, but around the 1,000. As at the Passion Play, all manner of things were well . . .

Perhaps some people preferred the first: because, as a friend bluntly put it, "it was a murder story".

You've no idea, though, the difficulty that some people

experienced in attending a Religious Play at all. Tibby, for instance: the kindest of neighbours. Flo told me she had the greatest difficulty in getting him into the grounds. For about twenty

minutes he waited at the entrance, to see if other men would go in. Then, at length, he plucked up courage. And sat, stiffly, and nervously, as he waited for the Play to begin. But all this was last time, at Easter. Now, the ice has been broken. Those who came were more than those who stayed away. The non-attendants were in the minority!

And one picks up little snatches of conversation on the grapevine. 'I hear the play has been

discussed favourably down the Mines' one man told me. Three ladies, I was told by another walked away from our Easter Play. Normally, the three of them went into

the pub for a drink: but this time (so my friend noticed) one of them walked past the bar door. 'Here', shouted her two friends. 'What about our drink?' 'Oh, not tonight' she replied: 'If you don't mind, not tonight'.

The other two nodded in agreement. And the three of them walked home together. Or, most touching of all, one hefty Australian at the bar to one of his mates. "What did you think of the Play, then?" "B .... Mighty!" came the reply.

'200' miles from home: a good chance to pack off thank-you letters so that at twelve or one tomorrow, I'll be ready to slip straight into the harness left these three weeks in other hands . . .

Saw Capt. Cook's cottage in Melbourne, shipped out here and put together piece by piece. Even helped start a Youth Club, and with the help of Penny across the road, put on for Randal's Sunday School our Collinsville Christmas Play.

Captain Cook's Cottage
which I see with Frank and Penny (Holt)...
16·12·65.

to from Myuna, 9/10 from imagination...
on Friday.

Myuna Cattle Station Jan 13 '66

Ready to celebrate Communion for Tom and Gloria and
Jennifer tomorrow. Canasta again tonight. Little Jenny is
confirmed now. And will soon go to school in Collinsville.
Up till now her Mother has
taught her at home: always a
problem for the "bush"
children, this schooling. I prepared Jenny for her Confirmation individually, as I think I
told you: and had a little service

of blessing when she was given a crucifix which she likes very much.

Two thirds of Collinsville still away on holiday. So I've been able to write our next Passion Play, around the character of the Penitent Thief. You need to have a sort of compère, always on the stage or by its side, if only to act as go-between for the actors and the audience . . . keep the children in order (300 sitting on the grass in front, and liable to laugh at the wrong moments).

I spent all last week with John, rather depressed. Or, as I should say, arranged for a series of friends to sit beside him and keep him company. Twenty-four hours a day at first, then twenty, then eighteen, at length down to two or three.

Little Kathy of the Sunday School came in last week to practise a lesson she was to read in church. She saw your drawing, Juliet, and said with surprise. "Your Sister can draw better than you, Brother!" Sic Transit Gloria Mundi.

The cows are still a nuisance beneath the Rectory. I'd picked two crate-fulls of mangoes: which I'd intended sending to clergy in cooler districts. But the cows came in while I was away visiting: and though the mangoes I had picked were purposely not quite ripe, they had chewed about half of them: and slobbered over the rest. I rescued a few for private consumption (after washing!): but the clergy in cooler districts (or was it Helen and Ted who had moved away?) will have to go mango-less.

Cows beneath the Rectory..... the end of my mangoes

Jan 31 66 Collinsville

Retreat was, as expected, quiet and cool and restful. Chapter Meetings mercifully shorter than before. On Tuesday set out with Anthony (our youngest brother) and on the winding Palmerston Highway we met Brother Clive, coming back to teach in Ravenshoe. He stopped, and had a cup of tea by the side of the road. In happy mood, he left us and we waved good-bye as he fleeted away. Later at 10.30 p.m., after one puncture and long delays before a flooded road, I was baling out my car

(the water was about six inches high inside car): Using, ironically, the thermos top from which C. and A. and I had drunk our cups of tea. A voice from the dark hailed "Hallo Brother". But I was all right, thank-you, and didn't need to stay with his family in Townsville, as I had to stay at S. Mark's.

On hearing this Ted, our ex-butcher in Collinsville, remarked that a S. Mark's student had run into a timber lorry (jinker) up on the Tableland: a nasty accident which he himself had stopped for. But the ambulance was there. And there was nothing he could do to help. He had, however, noticed Clive's suitcase labelled "St. Mark's, Townsville". So poor Clive died, just three days after becoming a full brother. The first time a brother has died in action in S. Barnabas' sixty four years out here. . . .

Feb 66. C'ville.

I had rather a sad duty to perform recently. A young couple who are passing through, so to speak (recent visitors anyway) lost their baby. It was in the early days of pregnancy. And Matron said the baby was not yet 'viable': I think that is the expression she used. Even so, they felt they would like a Service: which I certainly would have wished anyway. So I drove round with a little casket (from Jack the Undertaker) and one of the nurses

took me to a cold storage room: where, from the cooler, a tiny form wrapped round and round and round in white cloth was taken out and placed in the casket.

116

I then drove the parents in my V.W. out to the Cemetery, where the three of us said prayers for the baby that was never born. We did not even know to say "He" or "She" . . . so I commended "this child" instead. A little grave was ready for us, but by having the Service this way I was able to spare them most of the expense: bar one small casket. Not that one should speak of money, in such a matter. . . .

C'ville. Feb 2 66

I suppose the most remarkable event of last week was the disappearance of my little friend M. At 6.00 a.m. on Wednesday a worried Mrs. M called in at my back door: "Is M. with you, Brother? His bed hasn't been slept in at all last night". He wasn't with me, as you'll have guessed: so a mystery was on. A mystery all the more perplexing in that he had disappeared in 200 yards of matter-of-fact "bush town", (for I'd said goodnight to him the previous night as we returned from a practice for our Passion Play). Had he been bitten by a snake, and stumbled into the long grass of our creek? Had he, horror of horrors, been "done in" by one of the new people in town? "You never know who's in town these days" Sergeant Bob hinted

darkly as he and Les and I prodded vigorously at various inoffending bushes and long grass. In the end it turned out that M. had run away from school: having left a note on his bed to

this effect. But not before Mrs. M. had examined various subterranean pipes and Boris had suggested to me by phone that we close down the Mine and all join in the search.

By now we were not so worried. He had simply run away, as apparently he'd told four or five boys at school the day before that he intended to do. But whether to "Gordon's water Hole" or anywhere else, no-one knew. The search party split up. A band of railwaymen work their way up the hills. Others go by Landrover to one water hole, others in the Rail Car to another. But dear M. was at none of these. He was in the hills, not far away, sitting quietly in the shade of a rock. The Sgt. and I,

walking along the furthest edge of the hill, saw from two miles away cars, and what seemed like people, converging in victory. M. was found! So it's back to M.'s house for a glass of beer, while I console his Mother in the kitchen. 'It's all over now. No need to go over it again. He's back.' And next Sunday, little M. served for me, as usual, at Holy Communion.

C'ville. Feb 28. 66.

No, we didn't have any special services for Christian Unity week. I think you go a bit far in saying that Collinsville has achieved Christian Unity already! Though in one sense of course you are right, so far as I am concerned. For I certainly regard Arthur Ryan and John and their respective families as part of ours': or, perhaps I should put it the other way round. And the feeling I am sure is entirely mutual.

It's hard to describe attitudes and frames of mind. But the little Convent School children are very loving and respectful to me. And seem to treat me as if I were Fr. Ryan's curate, say; and part of their own church. And curate, I should add—not

119

Feb 28. '66.

little convent school children

out of theological juniority (if there is such a word)—but simply because I'm a little younger.

No. I'm wrong about the Services! We did have one. Because John came to say Evensong with me. The first time, almost, I've had company at 6.00 p.m. (about) on a week-day. I asked if he had any Methodist prayers we could use. But he said: "No. Lets just say Evensong like you always do." So we knelt, or sat (I forget which) and said Evensong together.

C'ville. March 1966

Have been seeing little Nicholas in hospital recently. 3 or 4 times a day. Dorothy is very busy, but more important: it is disturbing for her to see him in, and for Nicholas to see her go. I have devised a way of saying good-bye to Nicholas: which is  not to say good-bye at all, but drift in and out during the day so he never thinks I am leaving him: but always expects me to turn up at any moment, and assumes I am always around. I hope I haven't annoyed poor Matron or got in her way too much! She said to me today "You seem to spend the whole day here."

N.B. I didn't annoy her, as I wondered at the time. Because when the time came for me to leave she said: "I hope the next man turns up as much as you've done."

'You seem to spend the whole day here'

Collinsville. March 13 '66

For all the fact I'm upside down, and in Australia, and all that, my weeks have a basic similarity of diet. Five lessons on Monday, one wedding yesterday, five hours writing an eight minute sermon, and mosquitoes everywhere.

I went to Mt. Coolon on Thursday. A rough ride, for the rain has washed away the earth, leaving deep cracks and gullies. I had lunch, en route, at Havilah. My usual port of call. But they were expecting me, as I had rung up beforehand to see if they needed bread (which they did not) or mail (which they did). From there to Coolon, past creeks whose names come from a different age. 'Hangman's Creek', 'Dead Man's Gully'; or, most annoying, the '5 mile', the '3 mile', the '2 mile'. '2 miles to where?' You ask and nobody seems to know.

I met two dingoes on the way, and had to stop the car, before they bounded away into the bush. 'Why didn't you run them down?' Jack reproached me. 'You could have got two quid each for their tails!'

The children and I had a glorious swim in the creek until supper. We drove through the bush and the scrub, young Doug directing me. Strange that with the temperature 115 degrees in Cyril's store there should be water about.

At eight we had our usual service. Three adults, twenty children, and me (or is it I?). And two amusingly bent candles, testifying to the heat they had undergone in Cyril's store.

Pamela, aged twelve, acts as my churchwarden, giving out the books: and helping me carry them over, after we've washed up the supper things. Torches always, in case of snakes. Little pinpricks of light as the various families come from their little 'humpies'. We start off with a hymn that we have practised earlier, sitting on the hotel step. I cannot sing too well, we have today no piano; so it is a case of the blind leading the blind.

"Got an itchy foot" says Pamela of
Mount Cooton, after lemon squash on Thursday.

Pamela, who helps me give out
the hymn books at Mt. Cooton.

'The Church's One Foundation
Is Jesus Christ Her Lord . . .

The bent candles are spluttering in the dark. One of the paraffin lamps fades out and Aunt Etty primes it furiously

'She is His New Creation
By Water and the Word . . .

Little Aborigine boys are running about in the back of the darkened hall, and quite distract the others

'From Heaven He came and sought her
To be his Holy Bride. . . .'

"Will you sit down, please?" And the congregation don't so
much sit as sprawl backwards in the old canvas chairs, used in the
film shows of the roaring thirties. I see their eyes peering at me
out of the half-darkness. Really, we shall have to do something
about those paraffin lamps. And I am quicker to the point than
in this rambling letter, or else the five year olds will be off and
away. It's the story of the Good Samaritan, it may be . . . and he
stops at the edge of a road worse even than that to Mt. Coolon;
surveying what appears to be a corpse.

And tomorrow is another day. Leave after school and visit 'Fig Tree' successfully this time, (no sticking in the creek). And a picnic lunch beneath the shade of a . . . tree, (I was going to say a Coolibah tree, but I doubt if it was). Two men come in from the neighbouring stockyards to join us.

I return at 4.30 p.m. In time for two of the three members of my "sketch" class: which functions happily underneath the Rectory on a Friday afternoon, without much help or interference from me.

The heat is bearable. But it *is* hard to work mentally after lunch. You feel so like sleep, and this is a mixed blessing. Because it dampens your chances somewhat for 11 p.m.

On Thursday, I have to compere the little Convent School's swimming Carnival . . .

Rae, by the way, is back from New Zealand. And tells me the cooler climate has made her put on a whole stone in weight. Goodness knows how fat I'll get when I return! But I expect Rae will soon lose those extra pounds. My thermometer registered 119 degrees recently: though that was on the tarmac and not, as the Post Office works it out "in the shade". But then, that is where one lives and walks and talks for a lot of the day: on the tarmac.

Even so, we've had some brief respites from the heat in the form of heavy rain. I go to Ethel's for lunch on Saturdays; and Bob had to drive me back (or at least insisted on doing so)  because the Creek was flooded. Rae also said, which rather touched me, she was very sorry I was leaving in June: as she had hoped I would marry her, when the time came. Lynn, her sister, is sad too: because she wanted me to marry her as well. If you see what I mean!

C'ville. April 3 66

Our Passion Play draws nigh. Frank, who plays 'Our Lord' in the play, has grown a beard. He is very concerned about my antics as the penitent thief, especially during Our Lord's agony in Gethsemane. He's probably right, though I'm conscious always of keeping the congregation alert and attentive. Nothing, not even my silly antics, is as irreverent as boredom. We settle the matter happily, after a long and heated discussion.

P.S.
I met little Roy on the corner of Sonoma St recently. He told me: 'I hear you're going to be crustified, Brother.' Are you sure, I said. But he was adamant, though aged only 5. Yes, he replied. All the kids at school are saying so. I don't think he can have been referring to our Passion Play, or Confirmation: because I tried genuinely to understand him. So I am left with a dilemma. Or is it a prophecy? 'CRUSTIFIED' was all I could get out of him!

P.P.S. Apparently Ted, one of our faithful disciples, has caused much amusement in the pub recently by saying "Brother says I've got to have more passion". What I had meant was, that my plump bespectacled little pensioner should say his *words* with passion, as if they were the most important words he'd ever have to say. But Ted's friends have seen in this a comedy I had not intended!

Also, I'd had great difficulty, as ever, in reminding the disciples to take off their wrist watches. Ted, or even Ian, checking the time during the Last Supper is not, perhaps, quite the thing!

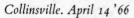

Our Play has come and gone again. If anything, even more happily than the previous time. And this despite a town apparently deserted on Good Friday morning. I saw hardly a soul, and only a bare (semi-bare) dozen graced the swimming pool.

But once again the children began to choose the front seats, an hour before the Play began. They laughed rather a lot during the Last Supper, which was unfortunate: and the Penitent Thief had to say "Ssh! or you'll give me away!" Also Peter's sword fell in half when he tried to cut off Malchus' ear . . . as it had done regularly in previous rehearsals. Only we hoped at last we'd mastered it.

Despite the apparently empty town, our thousand and more streamed in. Helped by cars from the bush, cars from Bowen:

even groups from Proserpine 100 miles away. Though one of
these hit a cow and came off worse. Frank the Dozer driver has
been so happy. I really think, for him at any rate, this Play must
feature as a highlight of his life. Having lived and talked the
play and nothing but the play for eight weeks, his joy is now
complete. And one has gently to bring him down from the
exultant heights, to the plebian but necessary business of day
to day living. Though F. has been more touched by the play
than most, if not all: the play does seem to have had more
effect than the others. Which is remarkable, since there cannot
have been more than 1400 people in town to begin with.
(The pub's takings were two thirds down on last year's.) The
stage too was remarkable. Being constructed at the Mine: and

the thief's heaven towered ten feet above the second highest
part for the final scene.

From here I had to warn them. "Careful as you go home now. I don't want you to join me here too soon! But you will come one day, won't you . . ."

C'ville. April 18 66

We had a nice service at Biralee yesterday. Frank (who is a Roman Catholic by the way) has long wanted to attend one of our services. So this formed as good an occasion as any. He came round beforehand to ask if he could come, and of course I was delighted. So duly, and very promptly, he turned up, his clean white shirt sparkling (if shirts can sparkle), and all his family ready, with room in the front seat for me. Off we went, only fifteen miles or so, and arrived to find Jeremy and Margaret there as well. So we had a pianist as well in Margaret, and a happy service followed by refreshments: and none of the traumatic experiences of Mt. Coolon!

C'ville. May 1 66

Anzac Day was a very sober affair by previous standards. I had taken over the Dawn Sermon, John being in Bowen: and I took it over fairly comfortably. Secure in the knowledge that a recitation of "Pooh Bear" would draw the same response and/or acclaim as anything else, from my swaying friends at 4.28

outside the Anzac Hall. As it was, they were in many cases stone cold sober, which un-nerved me considerably. One, however, was not: and after it was all over, he touched me rather, as he leant against the wall and regretted that it was my last Anzac. And saying, which would have made S. Paul turn in his grave, that I "had given the people the religion they wanted". I must add in my defence, that I'd never seen him in church: though he may possibly have glimpsed one of the plays.

However, I'm getting ahead of myself. I was up at 4.00 a.m. And about to change leisurely, when someone blew a long blast on the bugle. I went outside to find the Workers' Club opposite, which on previous occasions has been the scene of festive merry-making, in utter darkness. Since the March started from there at 4.25 I assumed they'd left early. Not knowing (1) That they were a reformed and sober lot this year (2) and anyway, they were still in bed.

I tore round to the Anzac Hall by car, sandals (no socks) in panic, to find . . . no one at all. And at 4.28 they still had not come. For Fred was vainly look-ing for the Drum, to beat time for them along the road. Even lunch was sober that day: although I'm told it brightened up considerably later on. But by that time I was at the hospital, christening Lionel John.

131

Beyond the grey stump
on Friday

Have just been out to say good-bye to Dick Nilon and his family at the Drill Camp. I shall miss them a lot, though of course I am due to move soon: and even further than these families with their little temporary group of huts, which go with a drill camp: and will I suppose be pulled up and moved (though I don't know) when the drilling is eventually finished.

Dick and his friends used to play tennis every Saturday afternoon, on his own home made court, made out of ant bed.

There's a little shack beside the court, where we would sit when spectating. And lots and lots of cold water (which became, in time, rather warm). I often used to play there. So did Jeff, from opposite the church: who had a favourite saying, whenever I hit a ball past him: "It's the Devil sitting on your shoulder, Brother". I am pleased in a way to relate that when the (supposedly) favourite Australian adjective is used (though not by anyone mentioned) in front of ladies: Joyce will cry out "Really, George. There are ladies present, you know". But my presence makes no difference at all, I am happy to say. Not that I get worked up in the slightest by words beginning with B. . . .

C'ville. May 17 '66

Q. When is a Service not a Service?
A. When it's at Mt. Coolon.

At least, so it seemed last Thursday. One of the lanterns still keeps going out. Carol, aged one and a half, completely dominated proceedings: the other children, four fifths of the congregation, found her much more interesting than me. But then, that is the same at Collinsville, when Neil plays with his collection money during the Sermon. Instead of leaving him alone, and listening to me, they all keep looking and 'ssshing'

and scolding at Neil: until I find it extremely hard to know what I'm talking about. The tunes, led by me, proved difficult at Mt. Coolon. In "O Jesus I have Promised" I kept wandering from one tune to another, but was able usually to finish the verse on some form of tune acceptable to all. And so, sluggishly, untunefully, and darkly, the Church Militant wended its way through another Thursday evening, on its journey to the City not built with hands.

The Rodeo was on Sunday. After Service I spent four and a half hours wandering round: renewing auld acquaintance, with people whom for the most part I had not seen for four or five days.

Aunt Etty of the outback.

My health keeps all right, thanks: though I do have this beastly toe, and have had to take Confirmation class in bed. Also I felt faint once at our Sunday Communion: so Boris our church-warden concelebrated. (I expect that's the word, it sounds right

anyway!). I sat, while Boris read the prayers: pronouncing only the forgiveness, and of course, saying the prayer of Consecration. I sat for most of the Service, and didn't preach. But managed to give my little family their Communion all right.

I've also, which pleased me very much, taken Les S. his Communion in hospital. I told him a little about the Service once or twice beforehand so he would not feel shy. He was

very happy too, and told me it was his first Communion since 1917.

N.B. I could hardly put this in a letter home (you know how Mothers worry) but the last 10 months, plus the next 1 or 2, almost constituted for me "the year of the toe". At least, I made an awful fuss about it: and unless you have ingrowing toe-nails yourself, you'll think me a dreadful coward, which perhaps I am. Anyway, what with having treatment, and then the nail off, and then the roots out, I wore a slipper with a hole in for months on end. And though Florence undoubtedly exaggerated when she said 'Brother's toe is the most famous toe in Collinsville': one year of my ministry there was what you might call a 'hopping Ministry'.

After this particular onslaught, by a visiting doctor, on my extremity: I had about 20 minutes after leaving the operating table before the effects of the local anaesthetic wore off. In that time I rushed back to collect my tooth-brush and pyjamas, and got to bed in Pat and Robin's house. (You have to keep the foot up: and they had an inside toilet.) So also had Dorothy and John, who took me in for another 4 or 5 days when Pat's family needed my bed. Then the Confirmation: which I sat through, with my foot up as best I could. I think I stood to present my four candidates.

I hope you never get ingrowing toe-nails. It makes you most irritable. When even in the early days little Christine inadvertently trod on my toe during Religious Instruction my thoughts were anything but religious. But I don't think I said anything.

My main difficulty, when I returned to the Rectory, was getting to the little hut at the bottom of the garden. I used my brooms upside down, as crutches, to help keep my foot up: which much intrigued Flo's little grand-daughter Kerry. Kerry saw me going up the path, broom-wise, and asked excitedly when it was all over. 'Nana. When's Brother going to do it again?' Kerry regarded my antics as the highlight of her day. But Flo' and Tibby were much more understanding.

C'ville. 20 June '66

There's been a tragic affair here: and the trouble is, you can do so little to help. Kay, a young girl from New Zealand, died in a car crash a week or so back. (I had in fact seen the Ambulance car come in, for I was late leaving hospital that night. But I'd assumed the two feet protruding from the back to be someone sick, and already in Kevin and the Doctor's good hands.) But the next day I heard: and went down to the Police Station to see what we could do. Apparently, the police have to notify Brisbane: which takes two days: before Brisbane can cable through to Kay's parents. By which time of course the two days may be three or four; and because of the heat poor Kay will already be buried. I used our Sunday collection of £7 to phone Greymouth, N.Z. myself (everyone in church of course agreeing and wishing they could do more). By great good luck I had the phone number of a friend of Kay's parents. So it was from a friend that they heard and not from an official. The friend phoned me back later at the Rectory. So we were at least able to arrange for Kay's body to be flown home. But as I say—I wish we could have done more.

It seems so wrong that aliens (and New Zealanders are aliens apparently) can be buried before the next of kin are told.

I've asked Boris to see if we can change the State law over this. I've already seen one letter from a local Minister (in our State Parliament) about it. But alas, I shall be away and with you (not alas about that!) long before anything is settled.

July 66

My little Ministry at Collinsville is over. I had, so far as possible, avoided special 'leaving services' or anything of that sort. But a little girl brought me a key-ring, some others a purse: and I have two lovely book-ends made of petrified wood (wood buried underground and turned to stone over the centuries). Bill pressed a $20 note into my hand, as I passed through his cattle station (we've changed to decimal currency, you notice) and the boys in the Band at our Fair that evening insisted on giving me their fee. I could not stop them. The next day our

Methodist Minister John (he was Herod in the Play) brought me a lovely book of photographs about Australia. Frank and his children gave me a book of Australian verse. And then Bert called with a bottle of wine, which he at once helped me drink by way of cele- (or conso-) lation at my going. Even so, there were *no* special services. Fr. Hare, my successor, must increase, and I must decrease.

I did in the end relent in a small way. For I'd a longing to celebrate early on the week-day of my departure. So I told someone the day before. Twenty-two came, and of these I think about fifteen I had prepared for Confirmation myself.

I phoned good-bye to a few friends. The phone here is really a very friendly instrument. "Is it Bernie you want?" says the operator. "Well, I'm afraid he's out and won't be back till tea". I usually ask for people's names rather than for their numbers. . . .

Then I went to say good-bye to Flo! And she, on opening the door, burst into tears. Until now I'd been too busy to realise properly that I was going. But now I knew. And did not know really what to say. And yet I was deeply moved by those tears: and thought, perhaps, despite all my weaknesses "it cannot be that the child of these tears should perish". Joyce and Dotty and one or two children were at the gate. I got into Dorothy's Holden, and I looked back

through the dust rising behind our car. Flo's front door was a third open and a white handkerchief was waving slightly.

I saw, through a mist, Keith waving from the door of his Cafe. Then we turned right, up past the Hospital and onto the dirt road. Little Nicholas was in the back of the car and asked his Mother: 'Why is Brother looking out of the window?' "Quiet, dear," she replied. "He's thinking".

P.S. A little later.
You'll be thinking Australia's a small place. I stopped in Brisbane, 900 miles from Collinsville: and met Norma's Granny, (Norma played 'Mary' in our Christmas Play) on a zebra crossing.

Later that day I had supper with Jean and Thom, Irish immigrants I'd last met two and a half years before. (They are settled now . . . soon to build their own house.) Thom said: 'There's a man in this block of flats whose brother was a Disciple in one of your Plays'. Then I visited a girl's school to say good-bye to Margaret of Bowen. Some other girls from the Ravenshoe district were there too. One of them pointed over the road. "See that house? The girl living there is the daughter of your Angel Gabriel."

This series of coincidences had not quite finished. At Sydney Airport, while waiting for my plane, I espied Marion: back from fourteen months nursing in Tasmania. She was the Serving Maid in our first play who made poor Peter's life such a misery.

She and I had a glass of orange squash (ridiculously expensive) together: she told me she was on her way back to Collinsville to marry Adrian. He had been one of our first recruits: the Roman Centurion who said "Truly. This was the Son of God".

P.P.S. On re-reading these letters, with the help of my diary, I realise only too strongly that they do not quite strike that apposite note of evangelic zeal which so characterised the letters of St. Paul. Where he wrote of Sin and Grace and Justification, I seem to write of earth closets, tennis with the children, and bathes in Little Milly. This is probably as well. Since what was said of one cleric is true of most: namely, that they are nice and even interesting people, provided you can keep them off religion.

Even so, to redress the balance, I end, as perhaps I should have begun, with a little bush sermon. . . .

I was visiting a little outback village once, away in North Queensland, when I saw on the reddish dust of the ground a straight black line, as if someone had marked it with a large pencil. I'd be exaggerating if I said it stretched away, as far as the eye could see. But it did in fact stretch quite a way. So I stooped down to see what it was. . . .

An army of black ants on the march. But I must confess, as I peered at them closely, they didn't appear very much like an army. Or if they did, it was an army of highly irregular soldiers. They seemed to be running round in circles. Some had food, others were trying to take it from them, some were pushing and barging, and all of them went in different directions. "Some army," I thought. But then I stood up, and from my six foot, or whatever, they seemed again like one great army. Marching in purposeful fashion across the Australian bush.

I sometimes wonder what a complete outsider, a man from Mars say, would make of the Christian Church. Supposing that he stooped down, as it were, and looked closely. Our divisions, at any rate, would be obvious. With noticeboards announcing the Parish Church of St. Botolph on one corner of the road, the Chapel of our Lady on the other, and the Free Church down the hill. But let's suppose he were to look even closer: at the life of a particular church. The Rector has a new scheme for raising money. The congregation are pretty well divided on the issue. The Council Meetings are in a quandary over the proposed Church hall. And the Choirmaster and Organist are at loggerheads over these modern hymn tunes. Some Army, the outsider would think: and then hum an old tune to different words:

"We are all divided—not one body we,
 Not much faith and doctrine—
 Not much charity."

And then he looks closer still: not at the individual church, but at individual Christians. It's the same story, I'm afraid. A nervous, irritable man, a rather pompous little woman; a bag of complexes and neuroses; trying to be good, with the contradictions of utter failure. Sincere attempts to follow Christ, coupled with blind spots and glaring sins.

So perhaps it is not unfair to ask him to stand up for a minute. For if you stand up, then you see the Church in perspective. Perhaps as Mankind herself in search of God—a great army, of all peoples, and colours and habits, tramping on down through the ages. Perhaps, more simply, as followers of the Carpenter, the one army of the living God: with the Cross of Jesus going on before.